▲

PRESENTED TO:

_____

BY:

_____

▼

_____ ▲▲▲

Y2J
Promise
Book

J. COUNTRYMAN
NASHVILLE
A Thomas Nelson Company

ISBN: 08499-5580-7

Printed in the United States of America

Contents

JESUS IS YOUR...

▼ ▼ ▼

SAVIOR

My spirit has rejoiced in God my Savior.

Luke 1:47

Being justified freely by His grace through the redemption that is in Christ Jesus, whom God set forth as a propitiation by His blood, through faith, to demonstrate His righteousness, because in His forbearance God had passed over the sins that were previously committed.

Romans 3:24, 25

Nevertheless He saved them for His name's sake, that He might make His mighty power known.

Psalm 106:8

But God demonstrates His own love toward us, in that while we were still sinners, Christ died for us.

Romans 5:8

For God did not send His Son into the world to condemn the world, but that the world through Him might be saved.

John 3:17

Most assuredly, I say to you, he who believes in Me has everlasting life.

John 6:47

▲ ▲ ▲

He who believes in the Son has everlasting life; and he who does not believe the Son shall not see life, but the wrath of God abides on him.

John 3:36

For by grace you have been saved through faith, and that not of yourselves; it is the gift of God, not of works, lest anyone should boast.

Ephesians 2:8, 9

Not by works of righteousness which we have done, but according to His mercy He saved us, through the washing of regeneration and renewing of the Holy Spirit, whom He poured out on us abundantly through Jesus Christ our Savior.

Titus 3:5, 6

Who has saved us and called us with a holy calling, not according to our works, but according to His own purpose and grace which was given to us in Christ Jesus before time began.

2 Timothy 1:9

And we have seen and testify that the Father has sent the Son as Savior of the world.

1 John 4:14

That if you confess with your mouth the Lord Jesus and believe in your heart that God has raised Him from the dead, you will be saved.

Romans 10:9

For the Son of Man has come to seek and to save that which was lost.

Luke 19:10

For God so loved the world that He gave His only begotten Son, that whoever believes in Him should not perish but have everlasting life.

John 3:16

But God, who is rich in mercy, because of His great love with which He loved us, even when we were dead in trespasses, made us alive together with Christ (by grace you have been saved).

Ephesians 2:4, 5

Therefore, if anyone is in Christ, he is a new creation; old things have passed away; behold, all things have become new.

2 Corinthians 5:17

LORD

That if you confess with your mouth the Lord Jesus and believe in your heart that God has raised Him from the dead, you will be saved. For with the heart one believes unto righteousness, and with the mouth confession is made unto salvation.

Romans 10:9, 10

Therefore let all the house of Israel know assuredly that God has made this Jesus, whom you crucified, both Lord and Christ.

Acts 2:36

For if we live, we live to the Lord; and if we die, we die to the Lord. Therefore, whether we live or die, we are the Lord's.

Romans 14:8

For You, LORD, are good, and ready to forgive, And abundant in mercy to all those who call upon You.

Psalm 86:5

For the Lord GOD will help Me; therefore I will not be disgraced. Therefore I have set My face like a flint, and I know that I will not be ashamed.

Isaiah 50:7

But it is good for me to draw near to God; I have put my trust in the Lord GOD, that I may declare all Your works.

Psalm 73:28

Blessed be the LORD, Who daily loads us with benefits.

Psalm 68:19

"And you shall love the LORD your God with all your heart, with all your soul, with all your mind, and with all your strength." This is the first commandment.

Mark 12:30

Therefore God also has highly exalted Him and given Him the name which is above every name, that at the name of Jesus every knee should bow, of those in heaven, and of those on earth, and of those under the earth, and that every tongue should confess that Jesus Christ is Lord, to the glory of God the Father.

Philippians 2:9–11

But why do you call Me "Lord, Lord", and do not do the things which I say?

Luke 6:46

LOVE

He who has My commandments and keeps them, it is he who loves Me. And he who loves Me will be loved by My Father, and I will love him and manifest Myself to him.

John 14:21

I love those who love me, and those who seek me diligently will find me.

Proverbs 8:17

The LORD has appeared of old to me, saying: "Yes, I have loved you with an everlasting love."

Jeremiah 31:3

And we have known and believed the love that God has for us. God is love, and he who abides in love abides in God, and God in him. We love Him because He first loved us.

1 John 4:16, 19

But God demonstrates His own love toward us, in that while we were still sinners, Christ died for us.

Romans 5:8

Beloved, let us love one another, for love is of God; and everyone who loves is born of God and knows God. He who does not love does not know God, for God is love. In this the love of God was manifested toward us, that God has sent His only begotten Son into the world, that we might live through Him. In this is love, not that we loved God, but that He loved us and sent His Son to be the propitiation for our sins. Beloved, if God so loved us, we also ought to love one another.

No one has seen God at any time. If we love one another, God abides in us, and His love has been perfected in us.

1 John 4:7–12

The LORD will command His loving kindness in the daytime, and in the night His song shall be with me.

Psalm 42:8

To know the love of Christ which passes knowledge; that you may be filled with all the fullness of God.

Ephesians 3:19

I will betroth you to Me forever; yes, I will betroth you to Me in righteousness and justice, in loving kindness and mercy.

Hosea 2:19

And now abide faith, hope, love, these three; but the greatest of these is love.

1 Corinthians 13:13

As the Father loved Me, I also have loved you; abide in My love.

If you keep My commandments, you will abide in My love, just as I have kept My Father's commandments and abide in His love.

These things I have spoken to you, that My joy may remain in you, and that your joy may be full.

This is My commandment, that you love one another as I have loved you.

Greater love has no one than this, than to lay down one's life for his friends.

These things I command you, that you love one another.

John 15:9–13, 17

JESUS IS YOUR
PEACE

Peace I leave with you, My peace I give to you; not as the world gives do I give to you. Let not your heart be troubled, neither let it be afraid.

John 14:27

The LORD will give strength to His people; the LORD will bless His people with peace.

Psalm 29:11

The things which you learned and received and heard and saw in me, these do, and the God of peace will be with you.

Philippians 4:9

Therefore, having been justified by faith, we have peace with God through our Lord Jesus Christ.

Romans 5:1

Be anxious for nothing, but in everything by prayer and supplication, with thanksgiving, let your requests be made known to God; and the peace of God, which surpasses all understanding, will guard your hearts and minds through Christ Jesus.

Philippians 4:6, 7

You will keep him in perfect peace, whose mind is stayed on You because he trusts in You.

Isaiah 26:3

I will both lie down in peace, and sleep; for You alone, O Lord, make me dwell in safety.

Psalm 4:8

And let the peace of God rule in your hearts, to which also you were called in one body; and be thankful.

Colossians 3:15

For unto us a Child is born, unto us a Son is given; and the government will be upon His shoulder. And His name will be called Wonderful, Counselor, Mighty God, Everlasting Father, Prince of Peace. Of the increase of His government and peace there will be no end, upon the throne of David and over His kingdom, to order it and establish it with judgment and justice from that time forward, even forever. The zeal of the Lord of hosts will perform this.

Isaiah 9:6, 7

For He Himself is our peace, who has made both one, and has broken down the middle wall of separation.

Ephesians 2:14

FORGIVENESS

As far as the east is from the west, so far has He removed our transgressions from us.

Psalm 103:12

If we confess our sins, He is faithful and just to forgive us our sins and to cleanse us from all unrighteousness.

1 John 1:9

For I will be merciful to their unrighteousness, and their sins and their lawless deeds I will remember no more.

Hebrews 8:12

Bearing with one another, and forgiving one another, if anyone has a complaint against another; even as Christ forgave you, so you also must do.

Colossians 3:13

And whenever you stand praying, if you have anything against anyone, forgive him, that your Father in heaven may also forgive you your trespasses.

Mark 11:25

"Come now, and let us reason together," says the LORD. "Though your sins are like scarlet, they shall be as white as snow; though they are red like crimson, they shall be as wool."

Isaiah 1:18

I, even I, am He who blots out your transgressions for My own sake;
And I will not remember your sins.

Isaiah 43:25

Blessed is he whose transgression is forgiven, whose sin is covered. Blessed is the man to whom the LORD does not impute iniquity, and in whose spirit there is no deceit.

Psalm 32:1, 2

Let the wicked forsake his way, and the unrighteous man his thoughts; let him return to the LORD, and He will have mercy on him; and to our God, for He will abundantly pardon.

Isaiah 55:7

Therefore, if anyone is in Christ, he is a new creation; old things have passed away; behold, all things have become new.

2 Corinthians 5:17

RIGHTEOUSNESS

And be found in Him, not having my own righteousness, which is from the law, but that which is through faith in Christ, the righteousness which is from God by faith.

Philippians 3:9

Even the righteousness of God, through faith in Jesus Christ, to all and on all who believe. For there is no difference.

Romans 3:22

And if Christ is in you, the body is dead because of sin, but the Spirit is life because of righteousness.

Romans 8:10

But of Him you are in Christ Jesus, who became for us wisdom from God—and righteousness and sanctification and redemption.

1 Corinthians 1:30

For He made Him who knew no sin to be sin for us, that we might become the righteousness of God in Him.

2 Corinthians 5:21

But to him who does not work but believes on Him who justifies the ungodly, his faith is accounted for righteousness.

Romans 4:5

For what the law could not do in that it was weak through the flesh, God did by sending His own Son in the likeness of sinful flesh, on account of sin: He condemned sin in the flesh, that the righteous requirement of the law might be fulfilled in us who do not walk according to the flesh but according to the Spirit.

Romans 8:3, 4

For whom He foreknew, He also predestined to be conformed to the image of His Son, that He might be the firstborn among many brethren. Moreover whom He predestined, these He also called; whom He called, these He also justified; and whom He justified, these He also glorified.

Romans 8:29, 30

The work of righteousness will be peace, and the effect of righteousness, quietness and assurance forever.

Isaiah 32:17

For with the heart one believes unto righteousness, and with the mouth confession is made unto salvation.

Romans 10:10

DELIVERER

And you shall know the truth, and the truth shall make you free. Therefore if the Son makes you free, you shall be free indeed.

John 8:32, 36

For the law of the Spirit of life in Christ Jesus has made me free from the law of sin and death.

Romans 8:2

The Spirit of the LORD is upon Me, because He has anointed Me to preach the gospel to the poor; He has sent Me to heal the brokenhearted, to proclaim liberty to the captives and recovery of sight to the blind, to set at liberty those who are oppressed.

Luke 4:18

Now the Lord is the Spirit; and where the Spirit of the Lord is, there is liberty.

2 Corinthians 3:17

But now having been set free from sin, and having become slaves of God, you have your fruit to holiness, and the end, everlasting life.

Romans 6:22

Beloved, do not believe every spirit, but test the spirits, whether they are of God; because many false prophets have gone out into the world. By this you know the Spirit of God: Every spirit that confesses that Jesus Christ has come in the flesh is of God, and every spirit that does not confess that Jesus Christ has come in the flesh is not of God. And this is the spirit of the Antichrist, which you have heard was coming, and is now already in the world. You are of God, little children, and have overcome them, because He who is in you is greater than he who is in the world.

1 John 4:1–4

Behold, I give you the authority to trample on serpents and scorpions, and over all the power of the enemy, and nothing shall by any means hurt you.

Luke 10:19

And these signs will follow those who believe: in My name they will cast out demons; they will speak with new tongues.

Mark 16:17

And they overcame him by the blood of the Lamb and by the word of their testimony, and they did not love their lives to the death.

Revelation 12:11

When you pass through the waters, I will be with you; and through the rivers, they shall not overflow you. When you walk through the fire, you shall not be burned, nor shall the flame scorch you.

Isaiah 43:2

But You, O LORD, are a shield for me, my glory and the One who lifts up my head.

Psalm 3:3

The eyes of the LORD run to and fro throughout the whole earth, to show Himself strong on behalf of those whose heart is loyal to Him.

2 Chronicles 16:9b

FELLOWSHIP

Therefore if there is any consolation in Christ, if any comfort of love, if any fellowship of the Spirit, if any affection and mercy, fulfill my joy by being like-minded, having the same love, being of one accord, of one mind.

Philippians 2:1, 2

He who has My commandments and keeps them, it is he who loves Me. And he who loves Me will be loved by My Father, and I will love him and manifest Myself to him.

John 14:21

For where two or three are gathered together in My name, I am there in the midst of them.

Matthew 18:20

That which we have seen and heard we declare to you, that you also may have fellowship with us; and truly our fellowship is with the Father and with His Son Jesus Christ.

1 John 1:3

Behold, I stand at the door and knock. If anyone hears My voice and opens the door, I will come in to him and dine with him, and he with Me.

Revelation 3:20

This is the message which we have heard from Him and declare to you, that God is light and in Him is no darkness at all. If we say that we have fellowship with Him, and walk in darkness, we lie and do not practice the truth. But if we walk in the light as He is in the light, we have fellowship with one another, and the blood of Jesus Christ His Son cleanses us from all sin.

1 John 1:5–7

God is faithful, by whom you were called into the fellowship of His Son, Jesus Christ our Lord.

1 Corinthians 1:9

Jesus answered and said to him, "If anyone loves Me, he will keep My word; and My Father will love him, and We will come to him and make Our home with him."

John 14:23

And walk in love, as Christ also has loved us and given Himself for us, an offering and a sacrifice to God for a sweet-smelling aroma. Speaking to one another in psalms and hymns and spiritual songs, singing and making melody in your heart to the Lord, giving thanks always for all things to God the Father in the name of our Lord Jesus Christ, submitting to one another in the fear of God.

Ephesians 5:2, 19–21

I am a companion of all who fear You, and of those who keep Your precepts.

Psalm 119:63

"Sing and rejoice, O daughter of Zion! For behold, I am coming and I will dwell in your midst," says the LORD.

Zechariah 2:10

Abide in Me, and I in you. As the branch cannot bear fruit of itself, unless it abides in the vine, neither can you, unless you abide in Me.

I am the vine, you are the branches. He who abides in Me, and I in him, bears much fruit; for without Me you can do nothing.

If you abide in Me, and My words abide in you, you will ask what you desire, and it shall be done for you.

John 15:4, 5, 7

EXAMPLE

Therefore be imitators of God as dear children. And walk in love, as Christ also has loved us and given Himself for us, an offering and a sacrifice to God for a sweet-smelling aroma.

Ephesians 5:1, 2

If I then, your Lord and Teacher, have washed your feet, you also ought to wash one another's feet. For I have given you an example, that you should do as I have done to you.

John 13:14, 15

By this we know love, because He laid down His life for us. And we also ought to lay down our lives for the brethren.

1 John 3:16

Now may the God of patience and comfort grant you to be like-minded toward one another, according to Christ Jesus, that you may with one mind and one mouth glorify the God and Father of our Lord Jesus Christ.

Therefore receive one another, just as Christ also received us, to the glory of God.

Romans 15:5–7

A new commandment I give to you, that you love one another; as I have loved you, that you also love one another.

John 13:34

Yet it shall not be so among you; but whoever desires to become great among you shall be your servant. And whoever of you desires to be first shall be slave of all. For even the Son of Man did not come to be served, but to serve, and to give His life a ransom for many.

Mark 10:43–45

Looking unto Jesus, the author and finisher of our faith, who for the joy that was set before Him endured the cross, despising the shame, and has sat down at the right hand of the throne of God.

For consider Him who endured such hostility from sinners against Himself, lest you become weary and discouraged in your souls.

Hebrew 12:2, 3

For to this you were called, because Christ also suffered for us, leaving us an example, that you should follow His step.

1 Peter 2:21

He who says he abides in Him ought himself also to walk just as He walked.

1 John 2:6

Let this mind be in you which was also in Christ Jesus.

And being found in appearance as a man, He humbled Himself and became obedient to the point of death, even the death of the cross.

Philippians 2:5, 8

God is able to make all grace abound toward you, that you, always having all sufficiency in all things, may have an abundance for every good work.

2 Corinthians 9:8

Blessed be the LORD, who daily loads us with benefits, the God of our salvation!

Psalm 68:19

COMPANION

No longer do I call you servants, for a servant does not know what his master is doing; but I have called you friends, for all things that I heard from My Father I have made known to you. You did not choose Me, but I chose you and appointed you that you should go and bear fruit, and that your fruit should remain, that whatever you ask the Father in My name He may give you.

John 15:15, 16

I am a companion of all who fear You,
And of those who keep Your precepts.

Psalm 119:63

A man who has friends must himself be friendly,
But there is a friend who sticks closer than a
brother.

Proverbs 18:24

Let your conduct be without covetousness; be content with such things as you have. For He Himself has said, "I will never leave you nor forsake you."

Hebrews 13:5

When my father and my mother forsake me,
Then the LORD will take care of me.

Psalm 27:10

I will not leave you orphans; I will come to you.
John 14:18

This is My commandment, that you love one another as I have loved you. Greater love has no one than this, than to lay down one's life for his friends. You are My friends if you do whatever I command you.

John 15:12–14

"For the mountains shall depart and the hills be removed, but My kindness shall not depart from you, nor shall My covenant of peace be removed," says the LORD, who has mercy on you.

Isaiah 54:10

But if we walk in the light as He is in the light, we have fellowship with one another, and the blood of Jesus Christ His Son cleanses us from all sin.

1 John 1:7

Now behold, two of them were traveling that same day to a village called Emmaus, which was seven miles from Jerusalem. And they talked together of all these things which had happened. So it was, while they conversed and reasoned, that Jesus Himself drew near and went with them.

Luke 24:13–15

BROTHER

For whoever does the will of My Father in heaven is My brother and sister and mother.

Matthew 12:50

Beloved, now we are children of God; and it has not yet been revealed what we shall be, but we know that when He is revealed, we shall be like Him, for we shall see Him as He is.

1 John 3:2

For as many as are led by the Spirit of God, these are sons of God.

Romans 8:14

And because you are sons, God has sent forth the Spirit of His Son into your hearts, crying out, "Abba, Father!" Therefore you are no longer a slave but a son, and if a son, then an heir of God through Christ.

Galatians 4:6, 7

For both He who sanctifies and those who are being sanctified are all of one, for which reason He is not ashamed to call them brethren.

Hebrews 2:11

For whom He foreknew, He also predestined to be conformed to the image of His Son, that He might be the firstborn among many brethren.

Romans 8:29

For you are all sons of God through faith in Christ Jesus.

Galatians 3:26

But as many as received Him, to them He gave the right to become children of God, to those who believe in His name.

John 1:12

Now, therefore, you are no longer strangers and foreigners, but fellow citizens with the saints and members of the household of God.

Ephesians 2:19

Behold what manner of love the Father has bestowed on us, that we should be called the children of God! Therefore the world does not know us, because it did not know Him.

1 John 3:1

GUARDIAN

For You have been a shelter for me, a strong tower from the enemy.

Psalm 61:3

For the eyes of the LORD are on the righteous, and His ears are open to their prayers; but the face of the LORD is against those who do evil. And who is he who will harm you if you become followers of what is good?

1 Peter 3:12, 13

So shall they fear
The name of the LORD from the west,
And His glory from the rising of the sun;
When the enemy comes in like a flood,
The Spirit of the LORD will lift up a standard
   against him.

Isaiah 59:19

But if you indeed obey His voice and do all that I speak, then I will be an enemy to your enemies and an adversary to your adversaries.

Exodus 23:22

But You, O Lord, are a shield for me,
My glory and the One who lifts up my head.

Psalm 3:3

When you pass through the waters, I will be with you; and through the rivers, they shall not overflow you. When you walk through the fire, you shall not be burned, nor shall the flame scorch you.

Isaiah 43:2

For the eyes of the Lord run to and fro throughout the whole earth, to show Himself strong on behalf of those whose heart is loyal to Him.

2 Chronicles 16:9a

But the Lord is faithful, who will establish you and guard you from the evil one.

2 Thessalonians 3:3

He will guard the feet of His saints, but the wicked shall be silent in darkness. For by strength no man shall prevail.

1 Samuel 2:9

SECURITY

Surely goodness and mercy shall follow me
All the days of my life;
And I will dwell in the house of the LORD
Forever.

Psalm 23:6

In Him you also trusted, after you heard the
word of truth, the gospel of your salvation; in
whom also, having believed, you were sealed with
the Holy Spirit of promise.

Ephesians 1:13

Blessed be the God and Father of our Lord
Jesus Christ, who according to His abundant
mercy has begotten us again to a living hope
through the resurrection of Jesus Christ from the
dead, to an inheritance incorruptible and undefiled and that does not fade away, reserved in
heaven for you, who are kept by the power of God
through faith for salvation ready to be revealed in
the last time.

1 Peter 1:3–5

And do not grieve the Holy Spirit of God, by
whom you were sealed for the day of redemption.
Ephesians 4:30

My sheep hear My voice, and I know them, and they follow Me. And I give them eternal life, and they shall never perish; neither shall anyone snatch them out of My hand. My Father, who has given them to Me, is greater than all; and no one is able to snatch them out of My Father's hand.

John 10:27–29

For I am persuaded that neither death nor life, nor angels nor principalities nor powers, nor things present nor things to come, nor height nor depth, nor any other created thing, shall be able to separate us from the love of God which is in Christ Jesus our Lord.

Romans 8:38, 39

All that the Father gives Me will come to Me, and the one who comes to Me I will by no means cast out.

John 6:37

Being confident of this very thing, that He who has begun a good work in you will complete it until the day of Jesus Christ.

Philippians 1:6

Do not labor for the food which perishes, but for the food which endures to everlasting life, which the Son of Man will give you, because God the Father has set His seal on Him.

John 6:27

Now to Him who is able to keep you from
     stumbling,
And to present you faultless
Before the presence of His glory with
     exceeding joy,
To God our Savior,
Who alone is wise,
Be glory and majesty,
Dominion and power,
Both now and forever.
Amen.

Jude 24, 25

SUFFICIENCY

And God is able to make all grace abound toward you, that you, always having all sufficiency in all things, may have an abundance for every good work.

2 Corinthians 9:8

Yet in all these things we are more than conquerors through Him who loved us.

Romans 8:37

Therefore I say to you, whatever things you ask when you pray, believe that you receive them, and you will have them.

Mark 11:24

Not that we are sufficient of ourselves to think of anything as being from ourselves, but our sufficiency is from God.

2 Corinthians 3:5

I can do all things through Christ who strengthens me.

Philippians 4:13

And whatever you ask in My name, that I will do, that the Father may be glorified in the Son.

John 14:13

And in that day you will ask Me nothing. Most assuredly, I say to you, whatever you ask the Father in My name He will give you. Until now you have asked nothing in My name. Ask, and you will receive, that your joy may be full.

John 16:23, 24

And He said to me, "My grace is sufficient for you, for My strength is made perfect in weakness." Therefore most gladly I will rather boast in my infirmities, that the power of Christ may rest upon me.

2 Corinthians 12:9

Bless the LORD, O my soul, and forget not all His benefits: Who forgives all your iniquities, Who heals all your diseases, Who redeems your life from destruction, Who crowns you with loving kindness and tender mercies.

Psalm 103:2–4

As His divine power has given to us all things that pertain to life and godliness, through the knowledge of Him who called us by glory and virtue, by which have been given to us exceedingly great and precious promises, that through these you may be partakers of the divine nature, having escaped the corruption that is in the world through lust.

2 Peter 1:3, 4

FULFILLMENT

Blessed are those who hunger and thirst for righteousness, for they shall be filled.

Matthew 5:6

Delight yourself also in the LORD, and He shall give you the desires of your heart.

Psalm 37:4

And Jesus said to them, "I am the bread of life. He who comes to Me shall never hunger, and he who believes in Me shall never thirst."

John 6:35

Jesus answered and said to her, "Whoever drinks of this water will thirst again, but whoever drinks of the water that I shall give him will never thirst. But the water that I shall give him will become in him a fountain of water springing up into everlasting life."

John 4:13, 14

My soul shall be satisfied as with marrow and fatness, and my mouth shall praise You with joyful lips. When I remember You on my bed, I meditate on You in the night watches.

Psalm 63:5, 6

The eyes of all look expectantly to You, and You give them their food in due season. You open Your hand and satisfy the desire of every living thing.

Psalm 145:15, 16

If you extend your soul to the hungry and satisfy the afflicted soul, then your light shall dawn in the darkness, and your darkness shall be as the noonday. The LORD will guide you continually, and satisfy your soul in drought, and strengthen your bones; you shall be like a watered garden, and like a spring of water, whose waters do not fail.

Isaiah 58:10, 11

The poor shall eat and be satisfied; those who seek Him will praise the LORD. Let your heart live forever!

Psalm 22:26

For He satisfies the longing soul, and fills the hungry soul with goodness.

Psalm 107:9

You shall eat in plenty and be satisfied, and praise the name of the LORD your God, Who has dealt wondrously with you; and My people shall never be put to shame.

Joel 2:26

EVERYTHING

Blessed be the God and Father of our Lord Jesus Christ, who has blessed us with every spiritual blessing in the heavenly places in Christ.

Ephesians 1:3

And whatever we ask we receive from Him, because we keep His commandments and do those things that are pleasing in His sight.

1 John 3:22

For to me, to live is Christ, and to die is gain.

Philippians 1:21

Blessed be the LORD,
Who daily loads us with benefits,
The God of our salvation!

Psalm 68:19

Now to Him who is able to do exceedingly abundantly above all that we ask or think, according to the power that works in us, to Him be glory in the church by Christ Jesus to all generations, forever and ever.

Ephesians 3:20, 21

And my God shall supply all your need according to His riches in glory by Christ Jesus.

Philippians 4:19

If you abide in Me, and My words abide in you, you will ask what you desire, and it shall be done for you.

John 15:7

Yet in all these things we are more than conquerors through Him who loved us.

Romans 8:37

Therefore let no one boast in men. For all things are yours: whether Paul or Apollos or Cephas, or the world or life or death, or things present or things to come—all are yours. And you are Christ's, and Christ is God's.

1 Corinthians 3:21–23

And whatever things you ask in prayer, believing, you will receive.

Matthew 21:22

THE WORD OF GOD
IS YOUR...

INFALLIBLE AUTHORITY

All Scripture is given by inspiration of God, and is profitable for doctrine, for reproof, for correction, for instruction in righteousness.

2 Timothy 3:16

Knowing this first, that no prophecy of Scripture is of any private interpretation, for prophecy never came by the will of man, but holy men of God spoke as they were moved by the Holy Spirit.

2 Peter 1:20, 21

For the word of God is living and powerful, and sharper than any two-edged sword, piercing even to the division of soul and spirit, and of joints and marrow, and is a discerner of the thoughts and intents of the heart.

Hebrews 4:12

You search the Scriptures, for in them you think you have eternal life; and these are they which testify of Me.

John 5:39

Forever, O LORD, Your word is settled in heaven.
Psalm 119:89

Every word of God is pure; He is a shield to those who put their trust in Him.

Proverbs 30:5

All flesh is as grass, and all the glory of man as the flower of the grass. The grass withers, and its flower falls away, but the word of the Lord endures forever. Now this is the word which by the gospel was preached to you.

1 Peter 1:24, 25

For He spoke, and it was done; He commanded, and it stood fast.

Psalm 33:9

For as the rain comes down, and the snow
    from heaven,
And do not return there,
But water the earth,
And make it bring forth and bud,
That it may give seed to the sower
And bread to the eater,
So shall My word be that goes forth from
    My mouth;
It shall not return to Me void,
But it shall accomplish what I please,
And it shall prosper in the thing for which I
    sent it.

Isaiah 55:10, 11

THE WORD OF GOD IS YOUR
Deed of Inheritance

The Spirit Himself bears witness with our spirit that we are children of God, and if children, then heirs—heirs of God and joint heirs with Christ, if indeed we suffer with Him, that we may also be glorified together.

Romans 8:16, 17

In My Father's house are many mansions; if it were not so, I would have told you. I go to prepare a place for you. And if I go and prepare a place for you, I will come again and receive you to Myself; that where I am, there you may be also.

John 14:2, 3

Blessed be the God and Father of our Lord Jesus Christ, who according to His abundant mercy has begotten us again to a living hope through the resurrection of Jesus Christ from the dead, to an inheritance incorruptible and undefiled and that does not fade away, reserved in heaven for you.

1 Peter 1:3, 4

Wait on the LORD, and keep His way, and He shall exalt you to inherit the land; when the wicked are cut off, you shall see it.

Psalm 37:34

And whatever you do, do it heartily, as to the Lord and not to men, knowing that from the Lord you will receive the reward of the inheritance; for you serve the Lord Christ.

Colossians 3:23, 24

Then the King will say to those on His right hand, "Come, you blessed of My Father, inherit the kingdom prepared for you from the foundation of the world."

Matthew 25:34

That the Gentiles should be fellow heirs, of the same body, and partakers of His promise in Christ through the gospel.

Ephesians 3:6

To open their eyes, in order to turn them from darkness to light, and from the power of Satan to God, that they may receive forgiveness of sins and an inheritance among those who are sanctified by faith in Me.

Acts 26:18

So now, brethren, I commend you to God and to the word of His grace, which is able to build you up and give you an inheritance among all those who are sanctified.

Acts 20:32

And if you are Christ's, then you are Abraham's seed, and heirs according to the promise.

Galatians 3:29

For all the promises of God in Him are Yes, and in Him Amen, to the glory of God through us.

2 Corinthians 1:20

But as it is written:
"Eye has not seen, nor ear heard,
Nor have entered into the heart of man
The things which God has prepared for those
who love Him."

1 Corinthians 2:9

GUIDE FOR LIFE

Your word is a lamp to my feet and a light to my path.

Psalm 119:105

Then Jesus said to those Jews who believed Him, "If you abide in My word, you are My disciples indeed. And you shall know the truth, and the truth shall make you free."

John 8:31, 32

By which have been given to us exceedingly great and precious promises, that through these you may be partakers of the divine nature, having escaped the corruption that is in the world through lust.

2 Peter 1:4

I will instruct you and teach you in the way you should go; I will guide you with My eye.

Psalm 32:8

He restores my soul; He leads me in the paths of righteousness for His name's sake.

Psalm 23:3

Your ears shall hear a word behind you, saying, "This is the way, walk in it," whenever you turn to the right hand or whenever you turn to the left.

Isaiah 30:21

This Book of the Law shall not depart from your mouth, but you shall meditate in it day and night, that you may observe to do according to all that is written in it. For then you will make your way prosperous, and then you will have good success.

Joshua 1:8

As He spoke by the mouth of His holy prophets, who have been since the world began.

To give light to those who sit in darkness and the shadow of death, to guide our feet into the way of peace.

Luke 1:70, 79

The steps of a good man are ordered by the LORD, and He delights in his way.

Psalm 37:23

When you roam, they will lead you; when you sleep, they will keep you; and when you awake, they will speak with you. For the commandment is a lamp, and the law a light; reproofs of instruction are the way of life.

Proverbs 6:22, 23

STABLE FORCE

Heaven and earth will pass away, but My words will by no means pass away.

Matthew 24:35

The grass withers, the flower fades, but the word of our God stands forever.

Isaiah 40:8

My son, give attention to my words; incline your ear to my sayings. Do not let them depart from your eyes; keep them in the midst of your heart; for they are life to those who find them, and health to all their flesh.

Proverbs 4:20–22

God is our refuge and strength, a very present help in trouble.

Psalm 46:1

The name of the LORD is a strong tower; the righteous run to it and are safe.

Proverbs 18:10

For assuredly, I say to you, till heaven and earth pass away, one jot or one tittle will by no means pass from the law till all is fulfilled.

Matthew 5:18

What then shall we say to these things? If God is for us, who can be against us?

Romans 8:31

"For I am the LORD. I speak, and the word which I speak will come to pass; it will no more be postponed; for in your days, O rebellious house, I will say the word and perform it," says the Lord GOD.

Ezekiel 12:25

Blessed be the LORD, who has given rest to His people Israel, according to all that He promised.

1 Kings 8:56a

He also brought me up out of a horrible pit,
Out of the miry clay,
And set my feet upon a rock,
And established my steps.

Psalm 40:2

STRENGTH

That He would grant you, according to the riches of His glory, to be strengthened with might through His Spirit in the inner man, that Christ may dwell in your hearts through faith;

Ephesians 3:16, 17a

But those who wait on the LORD
Shall renew their strength;
They shall mount up with wings like eagles,
They shall run and not be weary,
They shall walk and not faint.

Isaiah 40:31

Therefore take up the whole armor of God, that you may be able to withstand in the evil day, and having done all, to stand.

Ephesians 6:13

The LORD is my light and my salvation;
Whom shall I fear?
The LORD is the strength of my life;
Of whom shall I be afraid?

Psalm 27:1

The LORD is my rock and my fortress and my deliverer; my God, my strength, in whom I will trust; my shield and the horn of my salvation, my stronghold.

Psalm 18:2

That you may walk worthy of the Lord, fully pleasing Him, being fruitful in every good work and increasing in the knowledge of God; strengthened with all might, according to His glorious power, for all patience and longsuffering with joy; giving thanks to the Father who has qualified us to be partakers of the inheritance of the saints in the light.

Colossians 1:10–12

And he said, "O man greatly beloved, fear not! Peace be to you; be strong, yes, be strong!" So when he spoke to me I was strengthened, and said, "Let my lord speak, for you have strengthened me."

Daniel 10:19

My soul melts from heaviness; strengthen me according to Your word.

Psalm 119:28

He gives power to the weak, and to those who have no might He increases strength.

Isaiah 40:29

WHAT TO DO WHEN YOU ARE...

IN NEED OF PEACE

You will keep him in perfect peace, whose mind is stayed on You, because he trusts in You.

Isaiah 26:3

Therefore, having been justified by faith, we have peace with God through our Lord Jesus Christ.

Romans 5:1

For the kingdom of God is not eating and drinking, but righteousness and peace and joy in the Holy Spirit. For he who serves Christ in these things is acceptable to God and approved by men. Therefore let us pursue the things which make for peace and the things by which one may edify another.

Romans 14:17–19

For to be carnally minded is death, but to be spiritually minded is life and peace.

Romans 8:6

Great peace have those who love Your law,
And nothing causes them to stumble.

Psalm 119:165

Now may the God of hope fill you with all joy and peace in believing, that you may abound in hope by the power of the Holy Spirit.

Romans 15:13

Finally, brethren, farewell. Become complete. Be of good comfort, be of one mind, live in peace; and the God of love and peace will be with you.

2 Corinthians 13:11

Peace I leave with you, My peace I give to you; not as the world gives do I give to you. Let not your heart be troubled, neither let it be afraid.

John 14:27

LORD, You will establish peace for us, for You have also done all our works in us.

Isaiah 26:12

For you shall go out with joy,
And be led out with peace;
The mountains and the hills
Shall break forth into singing before you,
And all the trees of the field shall clap their
hands.

Isaiah 55:12

GRIEVING

For the LORD has comforted His people,
And will have mercy on His afflicted.

Isaiah 49:13b

Now may our Lord Jesus Christ Himself, and our God and Father, who has loved us and given us everlasting consolation and good hope by grace, comfort your hearts and establish you in every good word and work.

2 Thessalonians 2:16, 17

Blessed are those who mourn, for they shall be comforted.

Matthew 5:4

The Spirit of the Lord GOD is upon Me, Because the LORD has anointed Me to preach good tidings to the poor; He has sent Me to heal the brokenhearted . . . to comfort all who mourn, to console those who mourn in Zion, to give them beauty for ashes, the oil of joy for mourning, the garment of praise for the spirit of heaviness; that they may be called trees of righteousness, the planting of the LORD, that He may be glorified.

Isaiah 61:1–3

O Death, where is your sting? O Hades, where is your victory?

The sting of death is sin, and the strength of sin is the law. But thanks be to God, who gives us the victory through our Lord Jesus Christ.

1 Corinthians 15:55–57

Let us therefore come boldly to the throne of grace, that we may obtain mercy and find grace to help in time of need.

Hebrews 4:16

So the ransomed of the LORD shall return, and come to Zion with singing, with everlasting joy on their heads. They shall obtain joy and gladness; sorrow and sighing shall flee away.

Isaiah 51:11

We are confident, yes, well pleased rather to be absent from the body and to be present with the Lord.

2 Corinthians 5:8

And God will wipe away every tear from their eyes; there shall be no more death, nor sorrow, nor crying. There shall be no more pain, for the former things have passed away.

Revelation 21:4

Fear not, for I am with you;
Be not dismayed, for I am your God.
I will strengthen you,
Yes, I will help you,
I will uphold you with My righteous right
hand.

Isaiah 41:10

I do not want you to be ignorant, brethren,
concerning those who have fallen asleep, lest you
sorrow as others who have no hope.

For if we believe that Jesus died and rose
again, even so God will bring with Him those who
sleep in Jesus.

1 Thessalonians 4:13, 14

Blessed be the God and Father of our Lord
Jesus Christ, the Father of mercies and God of all
comfort, who comforts us in all our tribulation,
that we may be able to comfort those who are in
any trouble, with the comfort with which we ourselves are comforted by God.

2 Corinthians 1:3, 4

DESERTED BY LOVED ONES

When my father and my mother forsake me,
Then the LORD will take care of me.

Psalm 27:10

Persecuted, but not forsaken; struck down,
but not destroyed.

2 Corinthians 4:9

For the LORD your God is a merciful God, He
will not forsake you nor destroy you, nor forget the
covenant of your fathers which He swore to them.

Deuteronomy 4:31

Because he has set his love upon Me, therefore
I will deliver him;
I will set him on high, because he has known
My name. He shall call upon Me, and I will answer
him; I will be with him in trouble; I will deliver him
and honor him.

Psalm 91:14, 15

Be strong and of good courage, do not fear nor
be afraid of them; for the LORD your God, He is the
One who goes with you. He will not leave you nor
forsake you.

Deuteronomy 31:6

Why are you cast down, O my soul? And why are you disquieted within me? Hope in God; for I shall yet praise Him, the help of my countenance and my God.

Psalm 43:5

And those who know Your name will put their trust in You; for You, LORD, have not forsaken those who seek You.

Psalm 9:10

Casting all your care upon Him, for He cares for you.

1 Peter 5:7

Teaching them to observe all things that I have commanded you; and lo, I am with you always, even to the end of the age.

Matthew 28:20

For the LORD will not forsake His people, for His great name's sake, because it has pleased the LORD to make you His people.

1 Samuel 12:22

In Need of Patience

But those who wait on the LORD Shall renew
    their strength;
They shall mount up with wings like eagles,
They shall run and not be weary,
They shall walk and not faint.

Isaiah 40:31

It is good that one should hope and wait
quietly for the salvation of the LORD.

Lamentations 3:26

But if we hope for what we do not see, we
eagerly wait for it with perseverance.

Romans 8:25

I waited patiently for the LORD; and He
inclined to me, and heard my cry.

Psalm 40:1

For whatever things were written before were
written for our learning, that we through the
patience and comfort of the Scriptures might have
hope. Now may the God of patience and comfort
grant you to be like-minded toward one another,
according to Christ Jesus.

Romans 15:4, 5

Rest in the LORD, and wait patiently for Him; do not fret because of him who prospers in his way, because of the man who brings wicked schemes to pass.

Psalm 37:7

Therefore do not cast away your confidence, which has great reward. For you have need of endurance, so that after you have done the will of God, you may receive the promise: "For yet a little while, and He who is coming will come and will not tarry."

Hebrews 10:35–37

Therefore we also, since we are surrounded by so great a cloud of witnesses, let us lay aside every weight, and the sin which so easily ensnares us, and let us run with endurance the race that is set before us.

Hebrews 12:1

The end of a thing is better than its beginning; the patient in spirit is better than the proud in spirit. Do not hasten in your spirit to be angry, for anger rests in the bosom of fools.

Ecclesiastes 7:8, 9

Wait on the LORD; be of good courage, and He shall strengthen your heart; wait, I say, on the LORD!

Psalm 27:14

IN NEED OF CONFIDENCE

So we may boldly say: "The LORD is my helper; I will not fear. What can man do to me?"

Hebrews 13:6

I can do all things through Christ who strengthens me.

Philippians 4:13

Yet in all these things we are more than conquerors through Him who loved us.

Romans 8:37

Therefore I rejoice that I have confidence in you in everything.

2 Corinthians 7:16

For the LORD will be your confidence, and will keep your foot from being caught.

Proverbs 3:26

Therefore do not cast away your confidence, which has great reward. For you have need of endurance, so that after you have done the will of God, you may receive the promise.

Hebrews 10:35, 36

Now this is the confidence that we have in Him, that if we ask anything according to His will, He hears us. And if we know that He hears us, whatever we ask, we know that we have the petitions that we have asked of Him.

1 John 5:14, 15

In whom we have boldness and access with confidence through faith in Him.

Ephesians 3:12

Beloved, if our heart does not condemn us, we have confidence toward God.

1 John 3:21

And the young men shall utterly fall,
But those who wait on the LORD
Shall renew their strength;
They shall mount up with wings like eagles,
They shall run and not be weary,
They shall walk and not faint.

Isaiah 40:31

EXPERIENCING FEAR

No evil shall befall you, nor shall any plague come near your dwelling; for He shall give His angels charge over you, to keep you in all your ways.

Psalm 91:10, 11

For God has not given us a spirit of fear, but of power and of love and of a sound mind.

2 Timothy 1:7

So we may boldly say: "The LORD is my helper; I will not fear. What can man do to me?"

Hebrews 13:6

Yea, though I walk through the valley of the shadow of death, I will fear no evil; for You are with me; Your rod and Your staff, they comfort me. You prepare a table before me in the presence of my enemies; You anoint my head with oil; my cup runs over.

Psalm 23:4, 5

Peace I leave with you, My peace I give to you; not as the world gives do I give to you. Let not your heart be troubled, neither let it be afraid.

John 14:27

Be of good courage, and He shall strengthen your heart, all you who hope in the LORD.

Psalm 31:24

He who dwells in the secret place of the Most High Shall abide under the shadow of the Almighty.

Psalm 91:1

There is no fear in love; but perfect love casts out fear, because fear involves torment. But he who fears has not been made perfect in love.

1 John 4:18

In God I have put my trust; I will not be afraid. What can man do to me?

Psalm 56:11

In righteousness you shall be established; You shall be far from oppression, for you shall not fear; and from terror, for it shall not come near you.

Isaiah 54:14

HAVING MARITAL PROBLEMS

And the LORD God said, "It is not good that man should be alone; I will make him a helper comparable to him."

Genesis 2:18

Therefore a man shall leave his father and mother and be joined to his wife, and they shall become one flesh.

Genesis 2:24

Husbands, love your wives, just as Christ also loved the church and gave Himself for her. So husbands ought to love their own wives as their own bodies; he who loves his wife loves himself. For this reason a man shall leave his father and mother and be joined to his wife, and the two shall become one flesh. Nevertheless let each one of you in particular so love his own wife as himself, and let the wife see that she respects her husband.

Ephesians 5:21, 25, 28, 31, 33

Let all bitterness, wrath, anger, clamor, and evil speaking be put away from you, with all malice.

And be kind to one another, tenderhearted, forgiving one another, just as God in Christ forgave you.

Ephesians 4:31, 32

And if it seems evil to you to serve the LORD, choose for yourselves this day whom you will serve, whether the gods which your fathers served that were on the other side of the River, or the gods of the Amorites, in whose land you dwell. But as for me and my house, we will serve the LORD.

Joshua 24:15

Husbands, likewise, dwell with them with understanding, giving honor to the wife, as to the weaker vessel, and as being heirs together of the grace of life, that your prayers may not be hindered.

1 Peter 3:7

Love does no harm to a neighbor; therefore love is the fulfillment of the law.

Romans 13:10

Finally, all of you be of one mind, having compassion for one another; love as brothers, be tenderhearted, be courteous; not returning evil for evil or reviling for reviling, but on the contrary blessing, knowing that you were called to this, that you may inherit a blessing. For "He who would love life and see good days, let him refrain his tongue from evil, and his lips from speaking deceit. Let him turn away from evil and do good; let him seek peace and pursue it.

1 Peter 3:8–11

Hatred stirs up strife, but love covers all sins.

Proverbs 10:12

Since you have purified your souls in obeying the truth through the Spirit in sincere love of the brethren, love one another fervently with a pure heart.

1 Peter 1:22

I will behave wisely in a perfect way. Oh, when will You come to me? I will walk within my house with a perfect heart.

Psalm 101:2

WHAT TO DO WHEN YOU ARE
Having Financial Trouble

The LORD is my shepherd; I shall not want.
Psalm 23:1

And my God shall supply all your need according to His riches in glory by Christ Jesus.
Philippians 4:19

Therefore do not worry, saying, "What shall we eat?" or "What shall we drink?" or "What shall we wear?" For after all these things the Gentiles seek. For your heavenly Father knows that you need all these things. But seek first the kingdom of God and His righteousness, and all these things shall be added to you.
Matthew 6:31–33

The young lions lack and suffer hunger; but those who seek the LORD shall not lack any good thing.
Psalm 34:10

This Book of the Law shall not depart from your mouth, but you shall meditate in it day and night, that you may observe to do according to all that is written in it. For then you will make your way prosperous, and then you will have good success.
Joshua 1:8

And all these blessings shall come upon you and overtake you, because you obey the voice of the LORD your God: "Blessed shall you be in the city, and blessed shall you be in the country. Blessed shall be the fruit of your body, the produce of your ground and the increase of your herds, the increase of your cattle and the offspring of your flocks. Blessed shall be your basket and your kneading bowl. Blessed shall you be when you come in, and blessed shall you be when you go out. The LORD will cause your enemies who rise against you to be defeated before your face; they shall come out against you one way and flee before you seven ways. The LORD will command the blessing on you in your storehouses and in all to which you set your hand, and He will bless you in the land which the LORD your God is giving you."

Deuteronomy 28:2–8

But this I say: He who sows sparingly will also reap sparingly, and he who sows bountifully will also reap bountifully. So let each one give as he purposes in his heart, not grudgingly or of necessity; for God loves a cheerful giver. And God is able to make all grace abound toward you, that you, always having all sufficiency in all things, may have an abundance for every good work.

2 Corinthians 9:6–8

"Bring all the tithes into the storehouse, that there may be food in My house, and try Me now in this," says the LORD of hosts, "if I will not open for you the windows of heaven and pour out for you such blessing that there will not be room enough to receive it and I will rebuke the devourer for your sakes, so that he will not destroy the fruit of your ground, nor shall the vine fail to bear fruit for you in the field," says the LORD of hosts. "And all nations will call you blessed, for you will be a delightful land," says the LORD of hosts.

Malachi 3:10–12

And the LORD will grant you plenty of goods, in the fruit of your body, in the increase of your livestock, and in the produce of your ground, in the land of which the LORD swore to your fathers to give you. The LORD will open to you His good treasure, the heavens, to give the rain to your land in its season, and to bless all the work of your hand. You shall lend to many nations, but you shall not borrow. And the LORD will make you the head and not the tail; you shall be above only, and not be beneath, if you heed the commandments of the LORD your God, which I command you today, and are careful to observe them.

Deuteronomy 28:11–13

You shall remember the LORD your God, for it is He who gives you power to get wealth, that He may establish His covenant which He swore to your fathers, as it is this day.

Deuteronomy 8:18

I pray that you may prosper in all things and be in health, just as your soul prospers.

3 John 2

I have been young, and now am old; yet I have not seen the righteous forsaken, nor his descendants begging bread.

Psalm 37:25

Give, and it will be given to you: good measure, pressed down, shaken together, and running over will be put into your bosom. For with the same measure that you use, it will be measured back to you.

Luke 6:38

PHYSICALLY SICK

Then Jesus went about all the cities and villages, teaching in their synagogues, preaching the gospel of the kingdom, and healing every sickness and every disease among the people.

Matthew 9:35

And the whole multitude sought to touch Him, for power went out from Him and healed them all.

Luke 6:19

Heal me, O LORD, and I shall be healed; save me, and I shall be saved, for You are my praise.

Jeremiah 17:14

Is anyone among you sick? Let him call for the elders of the church, and let them pray over him, anointing him with oil in the name of the Lord. And the prayer of faith will save the sick, and the Lord will raise him up. And if he has committed sins, he will be forgiven.

James 5:14, 15

Beloved, I pray that you may prosper in all things and be in health, just as your soul prospers.

3 John 2

My son, give attention to my words; incline your ear to my sayings. Do not let them depart from your eyes; keep them in the midst of your heart; for they are life to those who find them, and health to all their flesh.

Proverbs 4:20–22

"For I will restore health to you and heal you of your wounds," says the LORD.

Jeremiah 30:17a

He was wounded for our transgressions, He was bruised for our iniquities; the chastisement for our peace was upon Him, and by His stripes we are healed.

Isaiah 53:5

Who forgives all your iniquities, who heals all your diseases.

Psalm 103:3

The centurion answered and said, "Lord, I am not worthy that You should come under my roof. But only speak a word, and my servant will be healed."

Matthew 8:8

WHAT TO DO WHEN YOU ARE

EXPERIENCING TROUBLES IN YOUR LIFE

The LORD is good, a stronghold in the day of trouble; and He knows those who trust in Him.

Nahum 1:7

Though I walk in the midst of trouble, You will revive me; You will stretch out Your hand against the wrath of my enemies, and Your right hand will save me.

Psalm 138:7

Be anxious for nothing, but in everything by prayer and supplication, with thanksgiving, let your requests be made known to God; and the peace of God, which surpasses all understanding, will guard your hearts and minds through Christ Jesus.

Philippians 4:6, 7

Blessed be the God and Father of our Lord Jesus Christ, the Father of mercies and God of all comfort, who comforts us in all our tribulation, that we may be able to comfort those who are in any trouble, with the comfort with which we ourselves are comforted by God.

2 Corinthians 1:3, 4

For we do not have a High Priest who cannot sympathize with our weaknesses, but was in all points tempted as we are, yet without sin. Let us therefore come boldly to the throne of grace, that we may obtain mercy and find grace to help in time of need.

Hebrews 4:15, 16

And we know that all things work together for good to those who love God, to those who are the called according to His purpose.

Romans 8:28

I will lift up my eyes to the hills—from whence comes my help? My help comes from the LORD, Who made heaven and earth.

Psalm 121:1, 2

Let not your heart be troubled; you believe in God, believe also in Me.

John 14:1

We are hard pressed on every side, yet not crushed; we are perplexed, but not in despair; persecuted, but not forsaken; struck down, but not destroyed.

2 Corinthians 4:8, 9

I can do all things through Christ who strengthens me.

Philippians 4:13

In Despair

For His anger is but for a moment,
His favor is for life;
Weeping may endure for a night,
But joy comes in the morning.
I cried out to You, O LORD;
And to the LORD I made supplication:
What profit is there in my blood,
When I go down to the pit?
Will the dust praise You?
Will it declare Your truth?
Hear, O LORD, and have mercy on me;
LORD, be my helper!
You have turned for me my mourning into
    dancing;
You have put off my sackcloth and clothed me
    with gladness,
To the end that my glory may sing praise to
    You and not be silent.
O LORD my God,
I will give thanks to You forever.

Psalm 30:5, 8–12

And so, after he had patiently endured, he
obtained the promise.

Hebrews 6:15

For if you return to the LORD, your brethren and your children will be treated with compassion by those who lead them captive, so that they may come back to this land; for the LORD your God is gracious and merciful, and will not turn His face from you if you return to Him.

2 Chronicles 30:9

I know how to be abased, and I know how to abound. Everywhere and in all things I have learned both to be full and to be hungry, both to abound and to suffer need. I can do all things through Christ who strengthens me.

Philippians 4:12, 13

We are hard pressed on every side, yet not crushed; we are perplexed, but not in despair; persecuted, but not forsaken; struck down, but not destroyed. Therefore we do not lose heart. Even though our outward man is perishing, yet the inward man is being renewed day by day. For our light affliction, which is but for a moment, is working for us a far more exceeding and eternal weight of glory, while we do not look at the things which are seen, but at the things which are not seen. For the things which are seen are temporary, but the things which are not seen are eternal.

2 Corinthians 4:8, 9, 16–18

Let your conduct be without covetousness; be content with such things as you have. For He Himself has said, "I will never leave you nor forsake you." So we may boldly say: "The LORD is my helper; I will not fear. What can man do to me?"

Hebrews 13:5, 6

Finally, brethren, whatever things are true, whatever things are noble, whatever things are just, whatever things are pure, whatever things are lovely, whatever things are of good report, if there is any virtue and if there is anything praiseworthy—meditate on these things.

Philippians 4:8

He has not dealt with us according to our sins, nor punished us according to our iniquities. For as the heavens are high above the earth, so great is His mercy toward those who fear Him; as far as the east is from the west, so far has He removed our transgressions from us.

Psalm 103:10–12

And we have known and believed the love that God has for us. God is love, and he who abides in love abides in God, and God in him.

1 John 4:16

And let us not grow weary while doing good, for in due season we shall reap if we do not lose heart.

Galatians 6:9

WHAT THE BIBLE HAS TO SAY ABOUT...

THE RETURN OF CHRIST

For as the lightning comes from the east and flashes to the west, so also will the coming of the Son of Man be. Immediately after the tribulation of those days the sun will be darkened, and the moon will not give its light; the stars will fall from heaven, and the powers of the heavens will be shaken. Then the sign of the Son of Man will appear in heaven, and then all the tribes of the earth will mourn, and they will see the Son of Man coming on the clouds of heaven with power and great glory. And He will send His angels with a great sound of a trumpet, and they will gather together His elect from the four winds, from one end of heaven to the other.

Matthew 24:27, 29–31

Now the Spirit expressly says that in latter times some will depart from the faith, giving heed to deceiving spirits and doctrines of demons, speaking lies in hypocrisy, having their own conscience seared with a hot iron, forbidding to marry, and commanding to abstain from foods which God created to be received with thanksgiving by those who believe and know the truth.

1 Timothy 4:1–3

But I do not want you to be ignorant, brethren, concerning those who have fallen asleep, lest you sorrow as others who have no hope. For if we believe that Jesus died and rose again, even so God will bring with Him those who sleep in Jesus. For this we say to you by the word of the Lord, that we who are alive and remain until the coming of the Lord will by no means precede those who are asleep. For the Lord Himself will descend from heaven with a shout, with the voice of an archangel, and with the trumpet of God. And the dead in Christ will rise first. Then we who are alive and remain shall be caught up together with them in the clouds to meet the Lord in the air. And thus we shall always be with the Lord. Therefore comfort one another with these words.

1 Thessalonians 4:13–18

But know this, that in the last days perilous times will come: For men will be lovers of themselves, lovers of money, boasters, proud, blasphemers, disobedient to parents, unthankful, unholy, unloving, unforgiving, slanderers, without self-control, brutal, despisers of good, traitors, headstrong, haughty, lovers of pleasure rather than lovers of God, having a form of godliness but denying its power. And from such people turn away!

2 Timothy 3:1–5

Knowing this first: that scoffers will come in the last days, walking according to their own lusts, and saying, "Where is the promise of His coming? For since the fathers fell asleep, all things continue as they were from the beginning of creation. But, beloved, do not forget this one thing, that with the Lord one day is as a thousand years, and a thousand years as one day. The Lord is not slack concerning His promise, as some count slackness, but is longsuffering toward us, not willing that any should perish but that all should come to repentance. But the day of the Lord will come as a thief in the night, in which the heavens will pass away with a great noise, and the elements will melt with fervent heat; both the earth and the works that are in it will be burned up. Therefore, since all these things will be dissolved, what manner of persons ought you to be in holy conduct and godliness, looking for and hastening the coming of the day of God, because of which the heavens will be dissolved, being on fire, and the elements will melt with fervent heat? Nevertheless we, according to His promise, look for new heavens and a new earth in which righteousness dwells.

2 Peter 3:3, 4, 8–13

And there will be signs in the sun, in the moon, and in the stars; and on the earth distress of nations, with perplexity, the sea and the waves roaring; men's hearts failing them from fear and the expectation of those things which are coming on the earth, for the powers of heaven will be shaken. Then they will see the Son of Man coming in a cloud with power and great glory. Now when these things begin to happen, look up and lift up your heads, because your redemption draws near.

Luke 21:25–28

Behold, I tell you a mystery: We shall not all sleep, but we shall all be changed—in a moment, in the twinkling of an eye, at the last trumpet. For the trumpet will sound, and the dead will be raised incorruptible, and we shall be changed. For this corruptible must put on incorruption, and this mortal must put on immortality. So when this corruptible has put on incorruption, and this mortal has put on immortality, then shall be brought to pass the saying that is written: "Death is swallowed up in victory. O Death, where is your sting? O Hades, where is your victory?" The sting of death is sin, and the strength of sin is the law. But thanks be to God, who gives us the victory through our Lord Jesus Christ.

1 Corinthians 15:51–57

Now as He sat on the Mount of Olives, the disciples came to Him privately, saying, "Tell us, when will these things be? And what will be the sign of Your coming, and of the end of the age?" And Jesus answered and said to them: "Take heed that no one deceives you. For many will come in My name, saying, 'I am the Christ,' and will deceive many. And you will hear of wars and rumors of wars. See that you are not troubled; for all these things must come to pass, but the end is not yet. For nation will rise against nation, and kingdom against kingdom. And there will be famines, pestilences, and earthquakes in various places. All these are the beginning of sorrows. Then they will deliver you up to tribulation and kill you, and you will be hated by all nations for My name's sake. And then many will be offended, will betray one another, and will hate one another. Then many false prophets will rise up and deceive many. And because lawlessness will abound, the love of many will grow cold. But he who endures to the end shall be saved. And this gospel of the kingdom will be preached in all the world as a witness to all the nations, and then the end will come."

Matthew 24:3–14

Looking for the blessed hope and glorious appearing of our great God and Savior Jesus Christ.
Titus 2:13

Let not your heart be troubled; you believe in God, believe also in Me.

In My Father's house are many mansions; if it were not so, I would have told you. I go to prepare a place for you.

And if I go and prepare a place for you, I will come again and receive you to Myself; that where I am, there you may be also.

And where I go you know, and the way you know.

John 14:1–4

WHAT THE BIBLE HAS TO SAY ABOUT
GROWING SPIRITUALLY

But also for this very reason, giving all diligence, add to your faith virtue, to virtue knowledge, to knowledge self-control, to self-control perseverance, to perseverance godliness, to godliness brotherly kindness, and to brotherly kindness love. For if these things are yours and abound, you will be neither barren nor unfruitful in the knowledge of our Lord Jesus Christ.

2 Peter 1:5–8

Let the word of Christ dwell in you richly in all wisdom, teaching and admonishing one another in psalms and hymns and spiritual songs, singing with grace in your hearts to the Lord.

Colossians 3:16

That we should no longer be children, tossed to and fro and carried about with every wind of doctrine, by the trickery of men, in the cunning craftiness of deceitful plotting, but, speaking the truth in love, may grow up in all things into Him who is the head—Christ.

Ephesians 4:14, 15

Meditate on these things; give yourself entirely to them, that your progress may be evident to all.

1 Timothy 4:15

Being confident of this very thing, that He who has begun a good work in you will complete it until the day of Jesus Christ. And this I pray, that your love may abound still more and more in knowledge and all discernment, that you may approve the things that are excellent, that you may be sincere and without offense till the day of Christ.

Philippians 1:6, 9, 10

But we all, with unveiled face, beholding as in a mirror the glory of the Lord, are being transformed into the same image from glory to glory, just as by the Spirit of the Lord.

2 Corinthians 3:18

But grow in the grace and knowledge of our Lord and Savior Jesus Christ. To Him be the glory both now and forever.

2 Peter 3:18

Be diligent to present yourself approved to God, a worker who does not need to be ashamed, rightly dividing the word of truth.

2 Timothy 2:15

For this reason I bow my knees to the Father of our Lord Jesus Christ, from whom the whole family in heaven and earth is named, that He would grant you, according to the riches of His glory, to be strengthened with might through His Spirit in the inner man, that Christ may dwell in your hearts through faith; that you, being rooted and grounded in love, may be able to comprehend with all the saints what is the width and length and depth and height—to know the love of Christ which passes knowledge; that you may be filled with all the fullness of God.

Ephesians 3:14–19

Changing the World

You are the light of the world. A city that is set on a hill cannot be hidden. Nor do they light a lamp and put it under a basket, but on a lampstand, and it gives light to all who are in the house. Let your light so shine before men, that they may see your good works and glorify your Father in heaven.

Matthew 5:14–16

For whatever is born of God overcomes the world. And this is the victory that has overcome the world—our faith. Who is he who overcomes the world, but he who believes that Jesus is the Son of God?

1 John 5:4, 5

We are of God. He who knows God hears us; he who is not of God does not hear us. By this we know the spirit of truth and the spirit of error. And we have known and believed the love that God has for us. God is love, and he who abides in love abides in God, and God in him. Love has been perfected among us in this: that we may have boldness in the day of judgment; because as He is, so are we in this world.

1 John 4:6, 16, 17

Those who are wise shall shine Like the brightness of the firmament, and those who turn many to righteousness like the stars forever and ever.

Daniel 12:3

And He said to them, "Go into all the world and preach the gospel to every creature. He who believes and is baptized will be saved; but he who does not believe will be condemned. And these signs will follow those who believe: In My name they will cast out demons; they will speak with new tongues; they will take up serpents; and if they drink anything deadly, it will by no means hurt them; they will lay hands on the sick, and they will recover. So then, after the Lord had spoken to them, He was received up into heaven, and sat down at the right hand of God. And they went out and preached everywhere, the Lord working with them and confirming the word through the accompanying signs."

Mark 16:15–20

But you shall receive power when the Holy Spirit has come upon you; and you shall be witnesses to Me in Jerusalem, and in all Judea and Samaria, and to the end of the earth.

Acts 1:8

Now faith is the substance of things hoped for, the evidence of things not seen. For by it the elders obtained a good testimony. By faith we understand that the worlds were framed by the word of God, so that the things which are seen were not made of things which are visible. Who through faith subdued kingdoms, worked righteousness, obtained promises, stopped the mouths of lions, quenched the violence of fire, escaped the edge of the sword, out of weakness were made strong, became valiant in battle, turned to flight the armies of the aliens.

Hebrew 11:1–3, 33, 34

By this all will know that you are My disciples, if you have love for one another.

John 13:35

And I also say to you that you are Peter, and on this rock I will build My church, and the gates of Hades shall not prevail against it. And I will give you the keys of the kingdom of heaven, and whatever you bind on earth will be bound in heaven, and whatever you loose on earth will be loosed in heaven.

Matthew 16:18, 19

Unsaved Loved Ones

So they said, "Believe on the Lord Jesus Christ, and you will be saved, you and your household."

Acts 16:31

Even so it is not the will of your Father who is in heaven that one of these little ones should perish.

Matthew 18:14

The Lord is not slack concerning His promise, as some count slackness, but is longsuffering toward us, not willing that any should perish but that all should come to repentance.

2 Peter 3:9

Cast your burden on the LORD, and He shall sustain you; He shall never permit the righteous to be moved.

Psalm 55:22

Train up a child in the way he should go,
And when he is old he will not depart from it.

Proverbs 22:6

Who will tell you words by which you and all your household will be saved.

Acts 11:14

Nevertheless I tell you the truth. It is to your advantage that I go away; for if I do not go away, the Helper will not come to you; but if I depart, I will send Him to you. And when He has come, He will convict the world of sin, and of righteousness, and of judgment.

John 16:7, 8

Who among you fears the LORD? Who obeys the voice of His Servant? Who walks in darkness And has no light? Let him trust in the name of the LORD and rely upon his God.

Isaiah 50:10

And a woman who has a husband who does not believe, if he is willing to live with her, let her not divorce him. For the unbelieving husband is sanctified by the wife, and the unbelieving wife is sanctified by the husband; otherwise your children would be unclean, but now they are holy. But if the unbeliever departs, let him depart; a brother or a sister is not under bondage in such cases. But God has called us to peace. For how do you know, O wife, whether you will save your husband? Or how do you know, O husband, whether you will save your wife?

1 Corinthians 7:13–16

The LORD has made known His salvation; His righteousness He has revealed in the sight of the nations.

Psalm 98:2

I will pour water on him who is thirsty,
And floods on the dry ground;
I will pour My Spirit on your descendants,
And My blessing on your offspring;

Isaiah 44:3

Keep justice, and do righteousness, for My salvation is about to come, and My righteousness to be revealed.

Isaiah 56:1

FORGIVING OTHERS

For if you forgive men their trespasses, your heavenly Father will also forgive you. But if you do not forgive men their trespasses, neither will your Father forgive your trespasses.

Matthew 6:14, 15

Take heed to yourselves. If your brother sins against you, rebuke him; and if he repents, forgive him.

Luke 17:3

For this is commendable, if because of conscience toward God one endures grief, suffering wrongfully. For what credit is it if, when you are beaten for your faults, you take it patiently? But when you do good and suffer, if you take it patiently, this is commendable before God. For to this you were called, because Christ also suffered for us, leaving us an example, that you should follow His steps: "Who committed no sin, nor was deceit found in His mouth; who, when He was reviled, did not revile in return; when He suffered, He did not threaten, but committed Himself to Him who judges righteously."

1 Peter 2:19–23

And whenever you stand praying, if you have anything against anyone, forgive him, that your Father in heaven may also forgive you your trespasses.

Mark 11:25

Blessed are those who are persecuted for righteousness' sake, for theirs is the kingdom of heaven. Blessed are you when they revile and persecute you, and say all kinds of evil against you falsely for My sake. Rejoice and be exceedingly glad, for great is your reward in heaven, for so they persecuted the prophets who were before you.

Matthew 5:10–12

For we know Him who said, "Vengeance is Mine, I will repay," says the Lord. And again, "The LORD will judge His people."

Hebrews 10:30

Beloved, do not think it strange concerning the fiery trial which is to try you, as though some strange thing happened to you; but rejoice to the extent that you partake of Christ's sufferings, that when His glory is revealed, you may also be glad with exceeding joy. If you are reproached for the name of Christ, blessed are you, for the Spirit of glory and of God rests upon you. On their part He is blasphemed, but on your part He is glorified.

1 Peter 4:12–14

Do not be overcome by evil, but overcome evil with good.

Romans 12:21

Let all bitterness, wrath, anger, clamor, and evil speaking be put away from you, with all malice. And be kind to one another, tenderhearted, forgiving one another, just as God in Christ forgave you.

Ephesians 4:31, 32

But I say to you, love your enemies, bless those who curse you, do good to those who hate you, and pray for those who spitefully use you and persecute you.

Matthew 5:44

SPIRITUAL TRIALS

Beloved, do not think it strange concerning the fiery trial which is to try you, as though some strange thing happened to you; but rejoice to the extent that you partake of Christ's sufferings, that when His glory is revealed, you may also be glad with exceeding joy. Yet if anyone suffers as a Christian, let him not be ashamed, but let him glorify God in this matter.

1 Peter 4:12, 13, 16

In You, O LORD, I put my trust; let me never be ashamed; deliver me in Your righteousness. Bow down Your ear to me, deliver me speedily; be my rock of refuge, a fortress of defense to save me. For You are my rock and my fortress; therefore, for Your name's sake, lead me and guide me. Pull me out of the net which they have secretly laid for me, for You are my strength. Into Your hand I commit my spirit; You have redeemed me, O LORD God of truth. I will be glad and rejoice in Your mercy, for You have considered my trouble; You have known my soul in adversities, and have not shut me up into the hand of the enemy; You have set my feet in a wide place.

Psalm 31:1–5, 7, 8

Cast your burden on the LORD, And He shall sustain you; He shall never permit the righteous to be moved.

Psalm 55:22

Create in me a clean heart, O God, and renew a steadfast spirit within me. Do not cast me away from Your presence, and do not take Your Holy Spirit from me. Restore to me the joy of Your salvation, and uphold me by Your generous Spirit. The sacrifices of God are a broken spirit, a broken and a contrite heart—these, O God, You will not despise.

Psalm 51:10–12, 17

The LORD has chastened me severely, but He has not given me over to death. Open to me the gates of righteousness; I will go through them, and I will praise the LORD. This is the gate of the LORD through which the righteous shall enter. I will praise You, for You have answered me, and have become my salvation.

Psalm 118:18–21

It is good for me that I have been afflicted, that I may learn Your statutes. Let, I pray, Your merciful kindness be for my comfort, according to Your word to Your servant.

Let Your tender mercies come to me, that I may live; for Your law is my delight.

Psalm 119:71, 76, 77

But He knows the way that I take; when He has tested me, I shall come forth as gold. My foot has held fast to His steps; I have kept His way and not turned aside.

Job 23:10, 11

In God I have put my trust; I will not be afraid. What can man do to me? Vows made to You are binding upon me, O God; I will render praises to You, for You have delivered my soul from death. Have You not kept my feet from falling, that I may walk before God In the light of the living?

Psalm 56:11–13

Why are you cast down, O my soul? And why are you disquieted within me? Hope in God; for I shall yet praise Him, the help of my countenance and my God.

Psalm 43:5

For You will light my lamp; the LORD my God will enlighten my darkness. For by You I can run against a troop, by my God I can leap over a wall. As for God, His way is perfect; the word of the LORD is proven; He is a shield to all who trust in Him. It is God who arms me with strength, and makes my way perfect.

Psalm 18:28–30, 32

GOD'S DIVINE PROTECTION

The LORD is my light and my salvation; whom shall I fear? The LORD is the strength of my life; of whom shall I be afraid? For in the time of trouble He shall hide me in His pavilion; in the secret place of His tabernacle He shall hide me; He shall set me high upon a rock.

Psalm 27:1, 5

But whoever listens to me will dwell safely,
And will be secure, without fear of evil.

Proverbs 1:33

The angel of the LORD encamps all around those who fear Him, and delivers them.

Psalm 34:7

I will both lie down in peace, and sleep;
For You alone, O LORD, make me dwell in safety.

Psalm 4:8

The fear of man brings a snare, but whoever trusts in the LORD shall be safe.

Proverbs 29:25

Yea, though I walk through the valley of the shadow of death, I will fear no evil; for You are with me; Your rod and Your staff, they comfort me.

Psalm 23:4

Are not two sparrows sold for a copper coin? And not one of them falls to the ground apart from your Father's will. But the very hairs of your head are all numbered. Do not fear therefore; you are of more value than many sparrows.

Matthew 10:29–31

So shall they fear the name of the LORD from the west, and His glory from the rising of the sun; when the enemy comes in like a flood, the Spirit of the LORD will lift up a standard against him.

Isaiah 59:19

The beloved of the LORD shall dwell in safety by Him, Who shelters him all the day long; and he shall dwell between His shoulders. The eternal God is your refuge, and underneath are the ever-lasting arms; He will thrust out the enemy from before you, and will say, "Destroy!"

Deuteronomy 33:12, 27

He who dwells in the secret place of the Most High shall abide under the shadow of the Almighty. I will say of the LORD, "He is my refuge and my fortress; my God, in Him I will trust." Surely He shall deliver you from the snare of the fowler and from the perilous pestilence. He shall cover you with His feathers, and under His wings you shall take refuge; His truth shall be your shield and buckler. No evil shall befall you, nor shall any plague come near your dwelling; for He shall give His angels charge over you, to keep you in all your ways. In their hands they shall bear you up, lest you dash your foot against a stone. Because he has set his love upon Me, therefore I will deliver him; I will set him on high, because he has known My name. He shall call upon Me, and I will answer him; I will be with him in trouble; I will deliver him and honor him. With long life I will satisfy him, and show him My salvation.

Psalm 91:1–4, 10–12, 14–16

DEALING WITH SUFFERING

Therefore, since Christ suffered for us in the flesh, arm yourselves also with the same mind, for he who has suffered in the flesh has ceased from sin, that he no longer should live the rest of his time in the flesh for the lusts of men, but for the will of God. Beloved, do not think it strange concerning the fiery trial which is to try you, as though some strange thing happened to you; but rejoice to the extent that you partake of Christ's sufferings, that when His glory is revealed, you may also be glad with exceeding joy. If you are reproached for the name of Christ, blessed are you, for the Spirit of glory and of God rests upon you. On their part He is blasphemed, but on your part He is glorified. But let none of you suffer as a murderer, a thief, an evildoer, or as a busybody in other people's matters. Yet if anyone suffers as a Christian, let him not be ashamed, but let him glorify God in this matter. For the time has come for judgment to begin at the house of God; and if it begins with us first, what will be the end of those who do not obey the gospel of God?

1 Peter 4:1, 2, 12–17

The righteous cry out, and the LORD hears, and delivers them out of all their troubles. The LORD is near to those who have a broken heart, and saves such as have a contrite spirit. Many are the afflictions of the righteous, but the LORD delivers him out of them all.

Psalm 34:17–19

You therefore must endure hardship as a good soldier of Jesus Christ.

2 Timothy 2:3

Though He was a Son, yet He learned obedience by the things which He suffered. And having been perfected, He became the author of eternal salvation to all who obey Him.

Hebrews 5:8, 9

This is a faithful saying: For if we died with Him, we shall also live with Him. If we endure, we shall also reign with Him. If we deny Him, He also will deny us.

2 Timothy 2:11, 12

Therefore let those who suffer according to the will of God commit their souls to Him in doing good, as to a faithful Creator.

1 Peter 4:19

My brethren, take the prophets, who spoke in the name of the Lord, as an example of suffering and patience. Indeed we count them blessed who endure. You have heard of the perseverance of Job and seen the end intended by the Lord—that the Lord is very compassionate and merciful.

James 5:10, 11

But may the God of all grace, who called us to His eternal glory by Christ Jesus, after you have suffered a while, perfect, establish, strengthen, and settle you. To Him be the glory and the dominion forever and ever.

1 Peter 5:10, 11

But we see Jesus, who was made a little lower than the angels, for the suffering of death crowned with glory and honor, that He, by the grace of God, might taste death for everyone. For it was fitting for Him, for whom are all things and by whom are all things, in bringing many sons to glory, to make the captain of their salvation perfect through sufferings.

Hebrews 2:9, 10

SIGNS OF THE END TIMES

And Jesus answered and said to them: "Take heed that no one deceives you. For many will come in My name, saying, 'I am the Christ,' and will deceive many. And you will hear of wars and rumors of wars. See that you are not troubled; for all these things must come to pass, but the end is not yet. For nation will rise against nation, and kingdom against kingdom. And there will be famines, pestilences, and earthquakes in various places. All these are the beginning of sorrows. Then they will deliver you up to tribulation and kill you, and you will be hated by all nations for My name's sake. And then many will be offended, will betray one another, and will hate one another. Then many false prophets will rise up and deceive many. And because lawlessness will abound, the love of many will grow cold. But he who endures to the end shall be saved. And this gospel of the kingdom will be preached in all the world as a witness to all the nations, and then the end will come."

Matthew 24:4–14

So Christ was offered once to bear the sins of many. To those who eagerly wait for Him He will appear a second time, apart from sin, for salvation.

Hebrews 9:28

But you, beloved, remember the words which were spoken before by the apostles of our Lord Jesus Christ: how they told you that there would be mockers in the last time who would walk according to their own ungodly lusts. These are sensual persons, who cause divisions, not having the Spirit. But you, beloved, building yourselves up on your most holy faith, praying in the Holy Spirit, keep yourselves in the love of God, looking for the mercy of our Lord Jesus Christ unto eternal life.

Jude 17–21

Heaven and earth will pass away, but My words will by no means pass away.

Matthew 24:35

Knowing this first: that scoffers will come in the last days, walking according to their own lusts, and saying, "Where is the promise of His coming?" For since the fathers fell asleep, all things continue as they were from the beginning of creation. But, beloved, do not forget this one thing, that with the Lord one day is as a thousand years, and a thousand years as one day. The Lord is not slack concerning His promise, as some count slackness, but is longsuffering toward us, not willing that any should perish but that all should come to repentance.

2 Peter 3:3, 4, 8–10

Then two men will be in the field: one will be taken and the other left. Watch therefore, for you do not know what hour your Lord is coming. Therefore you also be ready, for the Son of Man is coming at an hour you do not expect.

Matthew 24:40, 42, 44

But know this, that in the last days perilous times will come: For men will be lovers of themselves, lovers of money, boasters, proud, blasphemers, disobedient to parents, unthankful, unholy, unloving, unforgiving, slanderers, without self-control, brutal, despisers of good, traitors, head-strong, haughty, lovers of pleasure rather than lovers of God, having a form of godliness but denying its power. And from such people turn away!

2 Timothy 3:1–5

And it shall come to pass in the last days, says God, that I will pour out of My Spirit on all flesh; your sons and your daughters shall prophesy, your young men shall see visions, your old men shall dream dreams. And on My menservants and on My maidservants I will pour out My Spirit in those days; and they shall prophesy. I will show wonders in heaven above and signs in the earth beneath: The sun shall be turned into darkness, and the moon into blood, before the coming of the great and awesome day of the LORD. And it shall come to pass that whoever calls on the name of the LORD shall be saved.

Acts 2:17–21

Indeed the LORD has proclaimed to the end of the world: "Say to the daughter of Zion, 'Surely your salvation is coming; behold, His reward is with Him, and His work before Him.' And they shall call them The Holy People, The Redeemed of the Lord; and you shall be called Sought Out, A City Not Forsaken."

Isaiah 62:11, 12

For the time will come when they will not endure sound doctrine, but according to their own desires, because they have itching ears, they will heap up for themselves teachers; and they will turn their ears away from the truth, and be turned aside to fables.

2 Timothy 4:3, 4

THE LEADING OF THE LORD

A man's heart plans his way, but the LORD directs his steps. The lot is cast into the lap, but its every decision is from the LORD.

Proverbs 16:9, 33

Then He said, "Go out, and stand on the mountain before the LORD." And behold, the LORD passed by, and a great and strong wind tore into the mountains and broke the rocks in pieces before the LORD, but the LORD was not in the wind; and after the wind an earthquake, but the LORD was not in the earthquake; and after the earthquake a fire, but the LORD was not in the fire; and after the fire a still small voice.

1 Kings 19:11, 12

For the Son of Man has come to save that which was lost.

Matthew 18:11

The Lord is not slack concerning His promise, as some count slackness, but is longsuffering toward us, not willing that any should perish but that all should come to repentance.

2 Peter 3:9

For there are three that bear witness in heaven: the Father, the Word, and the Holy Spirit; and these three are one.

1 John 5:7

"For My thoughts are not your thoughts, nor are your ways My ways," says the LORD. "For as the heavens are higher than the earth, so are My ways higher than your ways, and My thoughts than your thoughts."

Isaiah 55:8, 9

If a trumpet is blown in a city, will not the people be afraid? If there is calamity in a city, will not the LORD have done it? Surely the Lord GOD does nothing, a lion has roared! Who will not fear? The Lord GOD has spoken! Who can but prophesy?

Amos 3:6–8

The LORD will guide you continually, and satisfy your soul in drought, and strengthen your bones; you shall be like a watered garden, and like a spring of water, whose waters do not fail.

Isaiah 58:11

I say to you that likewise there will be more joy in heaven over one sinner who repents than over ninety-nine just persons who need no repentance.

Luke 15:7

He found him in a desert land and in the wasteland, a howling wilderness; He encircled him, He instructed him, He kept him as the apple of His eye. As an eagle stirs up its nest, hovers over its young, spreading out its wings, taking them up, carrying them on its wings, so the LORD alone led him, and there was no foreign god with him.

Deuteronomy 32:10–12

THE JOY OF THE LORD

Nevertheless do not rejoice in this, that the spirits are subject to you, but rather rejoice because your names are written in heaven. In that hour Jesus rejoiced in the Spirit and said, "I thank You, Father, Lord of heaven and earth, that You have hidden these things from the wise and prudent and revealed them to babes. Even so, Father, for so it seemed good in Your sight."

Luke 10:20, 21

These things I have spoken to you, that My joy may remain in you, and that your joy may be full. This is My commandment, that you love one another as I have loved you.

John 15:11, 12

Do not sorrow, for the joy of the LORD is your strength.

Nehemiah 8:10b

This is the day the LORD has made; we will rejoice and be glad in it.

Psalm 118:24

A merry heart makes a cheerful countenance, but by sorrow of the heart the spirit is broken.

Proverbs 15:13

And you became followers of us and of the Lord, having received the word in much affliction, with joy of the Holy Spirit.

1 Thessalonians 1:6

But let all those rejoice who put their trust in You; let them ever shout for joy, because You defend them; let those also who love Your name be joyful in You. For You, O LORD, will bless the righteous; with favor You will surround him as with a shield.

Psalm 5:11, 12

Restore to me the joy of Your salvation, and uphold me by Your generous Spirit. Then I will teach transgressors Your ways, and sinners shall be converted to You.

Psalm 51:12, 13

Let the saints be joyful in glory; let them sing aloud on their beds.

Psalm 149:5

Come to Me, all you who labor and are heavy laden, and I will give you rest. Take My yoke upon you and learn from Me, for I am gentle and lowly in heart, and you will find rest for your souls. For My yoke is easy and My burden is light.

Matthew 11:28–30

THE FEAR OF THE LORD

The fear of the LORD is the beginning of wisdom, and the knowledge of the Holy One is understanding.

Proverbs 9:10

The fear of the LORD leads to life, and he who has it will abide in satisfaction; he will not be visited with evil.

Proverbs 19:23

The fear of the LORD is the beginning of knowledge, but fools despise wisdom and instruction.

Proverbs 1:7

In the fear of the LORD there is strong confidence, and His children will have a place of refuge. The fear of the LORD is a fountain of life, to turn one away from the snares of death.

Proverbs 14:26, 27

Let us hear the conclusion of the whole matter: Fear God and keep His commandments, for this is man's all. For God will bring every work into judgment, including every secret thing, whether good or evil.

Ecclesiastes 12:13, 14

Who is the man that fears the LORD? Him shall He teach in the way He chooses. He himself shall dwell in prosperity, and his descendants shall inherit the earth.

The secret of the LORD is with those who fear Him, and He will show them His covenant.

Psalm 25:12–14

In mercy and truth atonement is provided for iniquity; and by the fear of the LORD one departs from evil.

Proverbs 16:6

Praise the LORD! Blessed is the man who fears the LORD, who delights greatly in His commandments.

Psalm 112:1

The fear of the LORD prolongs days, but the years of the wicked will be shortened.

Proverbs 10:27

The LORD is righteous in all His ways, gracious in all His works. The LORD is near to all who call upon Him, to all who call upon Him in truth. He will fulfill the desire of those who fear Him; He also will hear their cry and save them.

Psalm 145:17–19

How to know...

YOU ARE BORN AGAIN

Most assuredly, I say to you, he who hears My word and believes in Him who sent Me has everlasting life, and shall not come into judgment, but has passed from death into life.

John 5:24

For by grace you have been saved through faith, and that not of yourselves; it is the gift of God, not of works, lest anyone should boast. For we are His workmanship, created in Christ Jesus for good works, which God prepared beforehand that we should walk in them.

Ephesians 2:8–10

Therefore whoever confesses Me before men, him I will also confess before My Father who is in heaven. And he who does not take his cross and follow after Me is not worthy of Me. He who finds his life will lose it, and he who loses his life for My sake will find it.

Matthew 10:32, 38–39

I have been crucified with Christ; it is no longer I who live, but Christ lives in me; and the life which I now live in the flesh I live by faith in the Son of God, who loved me and gave Himself for me.

Galatians 2:20

For you are all sons of God through faith in Christ Jesus. For as many of you as were baptized into Christ have put on Christ. There is neither Jew nor Greek, there is neither slave nor free, there is neither male nor female; for you are all one in Christ Jesus.

Galatians 3:26–28

I will give you a new heart and put a new spirit within you; I will take the heart of stone out of your flesh and give you a heart of flesh. I will put My Spirit within you and cause you to walk in My statutes, and you will keep My judgments and do them.

Ezekiel 36:26–27

Knowing this, that our old man was crucified with Him, that the body of sin might be done away with, that we should no longer be slaves of sin. For he who has died has been freed from sin. Now if we died with Christ, we believe that we shall also live with Him.

Romans 6:6–8

Put on the new man which was created according to God, in true righteousness and holiness.

Ephesians 4:24

And those who are Christ's have crucified the flesh with its passions and desires. If we live in the Spirit, let us also walk in the Spirit. Let us not become conceited, provoking one another, envying one another.

Galatians 5:24–25

Jesus answered and said to him, "Most assuredly, I say to you, unless one is born again, he cannot see the kingdom of God."

John 3:3

The Sufficiency of Jesus

And Jesus said to them, "I am the bread of life. He who comes to Me shall never hunger, and he who believes in Me shall never thirst."

John 6:35

And He said to me, "My grace is sufficient for you, for My strength is made perfect in weakness." Therefore most gladly I will rather boast in my infirmities, that the power of Christ may rest upon me.

2 Corinthians 12:9

And we have such trust through Christ toward God. Not that we are sufficient of ourselves to think of anything as being from ourselves, but our sufficiency is from God.

2 Corinthians 3:4–5

In Him was life, and the life was the light of men.

John 1:4

The LORD shall preserve you from all evil; He shall preserve your soul. The LORD shall preserve your going out and your coming in from this time forth, and even forevermore.

Psalm 121:7–8

Whom have I in heaven but You? And there is none upon earth that I desire besides You. My flesh and my heart fail; but God is the strength of my heart and my portion forever.

Psalm 73:25–26

For there is one God and one Mediator between God and men, the Man Christ Jesus.

1 Timothy 2:5

Jesus said to him, "I am the way, the truth, and the life. No one comes to the Father except through Me."

John 14:6

I am the good shepherd. The good shepherd gives His life for the sheep.

John 10:11

Therefore if the Son makes you free, you shall be free indeed.

John 8:36

The Way to Live in Christ

Let the word of Christ dwell in you richly in all wisdom, teaching and admonishing one another in psalms and hymns and spiritual songs, singing with grace in your hearts to the Lord.

Colossians 3:16

But be doers of the word, and not hearers only, deceiving yourselves.

James 1:22

Whoever transgresses and does not abide in the doctrine of Christ does not have God. He who abides in the doctrine of Christ has both the Father and the Son.

2 John 1:9

Looking unto Jesus, the author and finisher of our faith, who for the joy that was set before Him endured the cross, despising the shame, and has sat down at the right hand of the throne of God.

Hebrews 12:2

For all things are for your sakes, that grace, having spread through the many, may cause thanksgiving to abound to the glory of God. Therefore we do not lose heart. Even though our outward man is perishing, yet the inward man is being renewed day by day.

2 Corinthians 4:15–16

Abide in Me, and I in you. As the branch cannot bear fruit of itself, unless it abides in the vine, neither can you, unless you abide in Me. I am the vine, you are the branches. He who abides in Me, and I in him, bears much fruit; for without Me you can do nothing. If anyone does not abide in Me, he is cast out as a branch and is withered; and they gather them and throw them into the fire, and they are burned. If you abide in Me, and My words abide in you, you will ask what you desire, and it shall be done for you.

John 15:4–7

Now by this we know that we know Him, if we keep His commandments. He who says, "I know Him," and does not keep His commandments, is a liar, and the truth is not in him. But whoever keeps His word, truly the love of God is perfected in him. By this we know that we are in Him. He who says he abides in Him ought himself also to walk just as He walked.

1 John 2:3–6

Draw near to God and He will draw near to you. Cleanse your hands, you sinners; and purify your hearts, you double-minded.

James 4:8

I will meditate on Your precepts, and contemplate Your ways. I will delight myself in Your statutes; I will not forget Your word.

Psalm 119:15–16

Speaking to one another in psalms and hymns and spiritual songs, singing and making melody in your heart to the Lord, giving thanks always for all things to God the Father in the name of our Lord Jesus Christ.

Ephesians 5:19–20

YOU CAN RECOGNIZE EVIL

Beloved, do not believe every spirit, but test the spirits, whether they are of God; because many false prophets have gone out into the world. By this you know the Spirit of God: Every spirit that confesses that Jesus Christ has come in the flesh is of God, and every spirit that does not confess that Jesus Christ has come in the flesh is not of God. And this is the spirit of the Antichrist, which you have heard was coming, and is now already in the world.

1 John 4:1–3

"Behold, I am against those who prophesy false dreams," says the LORD, "and tell them, and cause My people to err by their lies and by their recklessness. Yet I did not send them or command them; therefore they shall not profit this people at all," says the LORD.

Jeremiah 23:32

For God is not the author of confusion but of peace, as in all the churches of the saints.

1 Corinthians 14:33

They profess to know God, but in works they deny Him, being abominable, disobedient, and disqualified for every good work.

Titus 1:16

He who sins is of the devil, for the devil has sinned from the beginning. For this purpose the Son of God was manifested, that He might destroy the works of the devil. Whoever has been born of God does not sin, for His seed remains in him; and he cannot sin, because he has been born of God.

1 John 3:8–9

For many deceivers have gone out into the world who do not confess Jesus Christ as coming in the flesh. This is a deceiver and an antichrist. Whoever transgresses and does not abide in the doctrine of Christ does not have God. He who abides in the doctrine of Christ has both the Father and the Son. If anyone comes to you and does not bring this doctrine, do not receive him into your house nor greet him; for he who greets him shares in his evil deeds.

2 John 1:7, 9–11

And when they say to you, "Seek those who are mediums and wizards, who whisper and mutter," should not a people seek their God? Should they seek the dead on behalf of the living? To the law and to the testimony! If they do not speak according to this word, it is because there is no light in them.

Isaiah 8:19–20

Beware of false prophets, who come to you in sheep's clothing, but inwardly they are ravenous wolves. You will know them by their fruits. Do men gather grapes from thornbushes or figs from thistles? Even so, every good tree bears good fruit, but a bad tree bears bad fruit. Therefore by their fruits you will know them. Not everyone who says to Me, "Lord, Lord," shall enter the kingdom of heaven, but he who does the will of My Father in heaven. Many will say to Me in that day, "Lord, Lord, have we not prophesied in Your name, cast out demons in Your name, and done many wonders in Your name?" And then I will declare to them, "I never knew you; depart from Me, you who practice lawlessness!"

Matthew 7:15–17, 20–23

For a good tree does not bear bad fruit, nor does a bad tree bear good fruit. For every tree is known by its own fruit. For men do not gather figs from thorns, nor do they gather grapes from a bramble bush.

Luke 6:43–44

A cunning Canaanite! Deceitful scales are in his hand; he loves to oppress.

Hosea 12:7

Freedom in Christ

There is therefore now no condemnation to those who are in Christ Jesus, who do not walk according to the flesh, but according to the Spirit. For the law of the Spirit of life in Christ Jesus has made me free from the law of sin and death.

Romans 8:1–2

There is neither Jew nor Greek, there is neither slave nor free, there is neither male nor female; for you are all one in Christ Jesus.

Galatians 3:28

Now the Lord is the Spirit; and where the Spirit of the Lord is, there is liberty.

2 Corinthians 3:17

And you shall know the truth, and the truth shall make you free. Therefore if the Son makes you free, you shall be free indeed.

John 8:32, 36

Stand fast therefore in the liberty by which Christ has made us free, and do not be entangled again with a yoke of bondage.

Galatians 5:1

For you, brethren, have been called to liberty; only do not use liberty as an opportunity for the flesh, but through love serve one another.

Galatians 5:13

For though I am free from all men, I have made myself a servant to all, that I might win the more.

1 Corinthians 9:19

I, Jesus, have sent My angel to testify to you these things in the churches. I am the Root and the Offspring of David, the Bright and Morning Star. And the Spirit and the bride say, "Come!" And let him who hears say, "Come!" And let him who thirsts come. Whoever desires, let him take the water of life freely.

Revelation 22:16–17

But he who looks into the perfect law of liberty and continues in it, and is not a forgetful hearer but a doer of the work, this one will be blessed in what he does.

James 1:25

For thus says the LORD: "You have sold yourselves for nothing, and you shall be redeemed without money."

Isaiah 52:3

WHEN YOUR LIFE IS CHRIST-CENTERED

You are My friends if you do whatever I command you. No longer do I call you servants, for a servant does not know what his master is doing; but I have called you friends, for all things that I heard from My Father I have made known to you. You did not choose Me, but I chose you and appointed you that you should go and bear fruit, and that your fruit should remain, that whatever you ask the Father in My name He may give you.

John 15:14–16

I will bless the LORD at all times; His praise shall continually be in my mouth. My soul shall make its boast in the LORD; the humble shall hear of it and be glad. Oh, magnify the LORD with me, and let us exalt His name together.

I sought the LORD, and He heard me, and delivered me from all my fears.

Psalm 34:1–4

In You, O LORD, I put my trust; let me never
  be put to shame.
For You are my hope, O Lord GOD; You are
  my trust from my youth.
Let my mouth be filled with Your praise and
  with Your glory all the day.

Psalm 71:1, 5, 8

Trust in Him at all times, you people; pour
out your heart before Him; God is a refuge for us.

Psalm 62:8

I will delight myself in Your statutes; I will not
  forget Your word.
Make me understand the way of Your precepts;
  so shall I meditate on Your wondrous works.

Psalm 119:16, 27

Then He said to them all, "If anyone desires
to come after Me, let him deny himself, and take
up his cross daily, and follow Me."

Luke 9:23–25

You will keep him in perfect peace, whose
mind is stayed on You, because he trusts in You.

Isaiah 26:3

O God, You are my God; early will I seek You; my soul thirsts for You; my flesh longs for You in a dry and thirsty land where there is no water.

So I have looked for You in the sanctuary, to see Your power and Your glory. My soul shall be satisfied as with marrow and fatness, and my mouth shall praise You with joyful lips. When I remember You on my bed, I meditate on You in the night watches. Because You have been my help, therefore in the shadow of Your wings I will rejoice.

Psalm 63:1–2, 5–7

It is good to give thanks to the LORD, and to sing praises to Your name, O Most High; to declare Your lovingkindness in the morning, and Your faithfulness every night.

Psalm 92:1–2

▲

GOD'S
PROMISES FOR
BELIEVERS...

▼

PROMISES OF TRUST

Therefore we will not fear, even though the earth be removed, and though the mountains be carried into the midst of the sea.

Psalm 46:2

But the salvation of the righteous is from the LORD; He is their strength in the time of trouble. And the LORD shall help them and deliver them; He shall deliver them from the wicked, and save them, because they trust in Him.

Psalm 37:39–40

Every word of God is pure; He is a shield to those who put their trust in Him.

Proverbs 30:5

The LORD redeems the soul of His servants, and none of those who trust in Him shall be condemned.

Psalm 34:22

Yes, we had the sentence of death in ourselves, that we should not trust in ourselves but in God who raises the dead, who delivered us from so great a death, and does deliver us; in whom we trust that He will still deliver us.

2 Corinthians 1:9–10

Uphold my steps in Your paths, that my footsteps may not slip. I have called upon You, for You will hear me, O God; incline Your ear to me, and hear my speech. Show Your marvelous lovingkindness by Your right hand, O You who save those who trust in You from those who rise up against them. Keep me as the apple of Your eye; hide me under the shadow of Your wings.

Psalm 17:5–8

He who heeds the word wisely will find good,
And whoever trusts in the LORD, happy is he.

Proverbs 16:20

The LORD is on my side; I will not fear. What can man do to me? It is better to trust in the LORD than to put confidence in man.

Psalm 118:6, 8

Those who trust in the LORD are like Mount Zion, which cannot be moved, but abides forever. Do good, O LORD, to those who are good, and to those who are upright in their hearts.

Psalm 125:1, 4

Whenever I am afraid,
I will trust in You.
In God (I will praise His word),
In God I have put my trust;
I will not fear.
What can flesh do to me?
In God I have put my trust;
I will not be afraid.
What can man do to me?
For You have delivered my soul from death.
Have You not kept my feet from falling,
That I may walk before God
In the light of the living?

Psalm 56:3–4, 11, 13

PROMISES OF CONTENTMENT

Let your conduct be without covetousness; be content with such things as you have. For He Himself has said, "I will never leave you nor forsake you." So we may boldly say: "The LORD is my helper; I will not fear. What can man do to me?"

Hebrews 13:5–6

There is therefore now no condemnation to those who are in Christ Jesus, who do not walk according to the flesh, but according to the Spirit. For the law of the Spirit of life in Christ Jesus has made me free from the law of sin and death. For those who live according to the flesh set their minds on the things of the flesh, but those who live according to the Spirit, the things of the Spirit. For to be carnally minded is death, but to be spiritually minded is life and peace.

Romans 8:1–2, 5–6

Not that I speak in regard to need, for I have learned in whatever state I am, to be content: I know how to be abased, and I know how to abound. Everywhere and in all things I have learned both to be full and to be hungry, both to abound and to suffer need. I can do all things through Christ who strengthens me.

Philippians 4:11–13

Now godliness with contentment is great gain. For we brought nothing into this world, and it is certain we can carry nothing out. And having food and clothing, with these we shall be content.

1 Timothy 6:6–8

Not that we are sufficient of ourselves to think of anything as being from ourselves, but our sufficiency is from God.

2 Corinthians 3:5

I will lift up my eyes to the hills. From whence comes my help? My help comes from the LORD, Who made heaven and earth. He will not allow your foot to be moved; He who keeps you will not slumber. The LORD is your keeper; the LORD is your shade at your right hand. The LORD shall preserve your going out and your coming in from this time forth, and even forevermore.

Psalm 121:1–3, 5, 8

You will keep him in perfect peace, whose mind is stayed on You, because he trusts in You.

Isaiah 26:3

And we know that all things work together for good to those who love God, to those who are the called according to His purpose.

Romans 8:28

Therefore do not worry, saying, "What shall we eat?" or "What shall we drink?" or "What shall we wear?" For after all these things the Gentiles seek. For your heavenly Father knows that you need all these things. But seek first the kingdom of God and His righteousness, and all these things shall be added to you. Therefore do not worry about tomorrow, for tomorrow will worry about its own things. Sufficient for the day is its own trouble.

Matthew 6:31–34

The Spirit Himself bears witness with our spirit that we are children of God, and if children, then heirs—heirs of God and joint heirs with Christ, if indeed we suffer with Him, that we may also be glorified together. For I consider that the sufferings of this present time are not worthy to be compared with the glory which shall be revealed in us.

Romans 8:16–18

PROMISES OF HOPE

Through the LORD's mercies we are not consumed, because His compassions fail not. They are new every morning; great is Your faithfulness. "The LORD is my portion," says my soul, "therefore I hope in Him."

Lamentations 3:22–24

Now may the God of hope fill you with all joy and peace in believing, that you may abound in hope by the power of the Holy Spirit.

Romans 15:13

Behold, the eye of the LORD is on those who fear Him, on those who hope in His mercy, to deliver their soul from death, and to keep them alive in famine. Our soul waits for the LORD; He is our help and our shield. For our heart shall rejoice in Him, because we have trusted in His holy name. Let Your mercy, O LORD, be upon us, just as we hope in you.

Psalm 33:18–22

You are my hiding place and my shield; I hope in Your word.

Psalm 119:114

And so, after he had patiently endured, he obtained the promise. That by two immutable things, in which it is impossible for God to lie, we might have strong consolation, who have fled for refuge to lay hold of the hope set before us. This hope we have as an anchor of the soul, both sure and steadfast, and which enters the Presence behind the veil.

Hebrews 6:15, 18–19

Do not be a terror to me; You are my hope in the day of doom.

Jeremiah 17:17

My soul, wait silently for God alone, for my expectation is from Him. He only is my rock and my salvation; He is my defense; I shall not be moved. In God is my salvation and my glory; the rock of my strength, and my refuge, is in God.

Psalm 62:5–7

I would have lost heart, unless I had believed that I would see the goodness of the LORD in the land of the living. Wait on the LORD; be of good courage, and He shall strengthen your heart; wait, I say, on the LORD!

Psalm 27:13–14

Or does He say it altogether for our sakes? For our sakes, no doubt, this is written, that he who plows should plow in hope, and he who threshes in hope should be partaker of his hope.

1 Corinthians 9:10

Therefore, having been justified by faith, we have peace with God through our Lord Jesus Christ, through whom also we have access by faith into this grace in which we stand, and rejoice in hope of the glory of God. And not only that, but we also glory in tribulations, knowing that tribulation produces perseverance and perseverance, character; and character, hope. Now hope does not disappoint, because the love of God has been poured out in our hearts by the Holy Spirit who was given to us.

Romans 5:1–5

PROMISES OF GOD'S NEVER ENDING LOVE

Then you will call upon Me and go and pray to Me, and I will listen to you. And you will seek Me and find Me, when you search for Me with all your heart.

Jeremiah 29:12–13

Draw near to God and He will draw near to you. Cleanse your hands, you sinners; and purify your hearts, you double-minded. Humble yourselves in the sight of the Lord, and He will lift you up.

James 4:8, 10

For everyone who asks receives, and he who seeks finds, and to him who knocks it will be opened. If you then, being evil, know how to give good gifts to your children, how much more will your heavenly Father give the Holy Spirit to those who ask Him!

Luke 11:10, 13

Blessed are those who keep His testimonies, who seek Him with the whole heart! With my whole heart I have sought You; oh, let me not wander from Your commandments!

Psalm 119:2, 10

Thus I will bless You while I live; I will lift up my hands in Your name. My soul shall be satisfied as with marrow and fatness, and my mouth shall praise You with joyful lips.

Psalm 63:4–5

Hear my cry, O God; attend to my prayer. From the end of the earth I will cry to You, when my heart is overwhelmed; lead me to the rock that is higher than I.

Psalm 61:1–2

All that the Father gives Me will come to Me, and the one who comes to Me I will by no means cast out.

John 6:37

You have made him to have dominion over the works of Your hands; You have put all things under his feet.

Psalm 18:6

The LORD is near to all who call upon Him, to all who call upon Him in truth.

Psalm 145:18

In the day when I cried out, You answered me, and made me bold with strength in my soul.

Psalm 138:3

PROMISES OF ETERNITY

Behold, the tabernacle of God is with men, and He will dwell with them, and they shall be His people. God Himself will be with them and be their God. And God will wipe away every tear from their eyes; there shall be no more death, nor sorrow, nor crying. There shall be no more pain, for the former things have passed away. Then He who sat on the throne said, "Behold, I make all things new." And He said to me, "Write, for these words are true and faithful." And He said to me, "It is done! I am the Alpha and the Omega, the Beginning and the End. I will give of the fountain of the water of life freely to him who thirsts."

Revelation 21:3–6

There are also celestial bodies and terrestrial bodies; but the glory of the celestial is one, and the glory of the terrestrial is another. So also is the resurrection of the dead. The body is sown in corruption, it is raised in incorruption. It is sown in dishonor, it is raised in glory. It is sown in weakness, it is raised in power. It is sown a natural body, it is raised a spiritual body. There is a natural body, and there is a spiritual body.

1 Corinthians 15:40, 42–44

The city had no need of the sun or of the moon to shine in it, for the glory of God illuminated it. The Lamb is its light. And the nations of those who are saved shall walk in its light, and the kings of the earth bring their glory and honor into it. Its gates shall not be shut at all by day (there shall be no night there). And they shall bring the glory and the honor of the nations into it. But there shall by no means enter it anything that defiles, or causes an abomination or a lie, but only those who are written in the Lamb's Book of Life.

Revelation 21:23–27

For since the beginning of the world men have not heard nor perceived by the ear, nor has the eye seen any God besides You, Who acts for the one who waits for Him.

Isaiah 64:4

And when I saw Him, I fell at His feet as dead. But He laid His right hand on me, saying to me, "Do not be afraid; I am the First and the Last. I am He who lives, and was dead, and behold, I am alive forevermore. Amen. And I have the keys of Hades and of Death."

Revelation 1:17–18

So when this corruptible has put on incorruption, and this mortal has put on immortality, then shall be brought to pass the saying that is written: "Death is swallowed up in victory. O Death, where is your sting? O Hades, where is your victory?" But thanks be to God, Who gives us the victory through our Lord Jesus Christ.

1 Corinthian 15:54, 55, 57

Violence shall no longer be heard in your land,
Neither wasting nor destruction within your
   borders;
But you shall call your walls Salvation,
And your gates Praise.
The sun shall no longer be your light by day,
Nor for brightness shall the moon give light
   to you;
But the LORD will be to you an everlasting light,
And your God your glory.
Your sun shall no longer go down,
Nor shall your moon withdraw itself;
For the LORD will be your everlasting light,
And the days of your mourning shall be ended.

Isaiah 60:18–20

But as it is written: "Eye has not seen, nor ear heard, nor have entered into the heart of man the things which God has prepared for those who love Him." But God has revealed them to us through His Spirit. For the Spirit searches all things, yes, the deep things of God. For what man knows the things of a man except the spirit of the man which is in him? Even so no one knows the things of God except the Spirit of God.

1 Corinthians 2:9–11

Surely goodness and mercy shall follow me all the days of my life; and I will dwell in the house of the LORD forever.

Psalm 23:6

He will swallow up death forever, and the Lord GOD will wipe away tears from all faces; the rebuke of His people He will take away from all the earth; for the LORD has spoken.

Isaiah 25:8

GOD'S PLAN OF
SALVATION

For all have sinned and fall short of the glory of God.

Romans 3:23

For the wages of sin is death, but the gift of God is eternal life in Christ Jesus our Lord.

Romans 6:23

But God demonstrates His own love toward us, in that while we were still sinners, Christ died for us.

Romans 5:8

For God so loved the world that He gave His only begotten Son, that whoever believes in Him should not perish but have everlasting life. For God did not send His Son into the world to condemn the world, but that the world through Him might be saved.

John 3:16, 17

That if you confess with your mouth the Lord Jesus and believe in your heart that God has raised Him from the dead, you will be saved. For with the heart one believes unto righteousness, and with the mouth confession is made unto salvation.

Romans 10:9, 10

For by grace you have been saved through faith, and that not of yourselves; it is the gift of God, not of works, lest anyone should boast.

Ephesians 2:8, 9

Therefore whoever confesses Me before men, him I will also confess before My Father who is in heaven.

Matthew 10:32

He who believes in the Son has everlasting life; and he who does not believe the Son shall not see life, but the wrath of God abides on him.

John 3:36

And this is the testimony: that God has given us eternal life, and this life is in His Son. He who has the Son has life; he who does not have the Son of God does not have life. These things I have written to you who believe in the name of the Son of God, that you may know that you have eternal life, and that you may continue to believe in the name of the Son of God.

1 John 5:11–13

Behold, I stand at the door and knock. If anyone hears My voice and opens the door, I will come in to him and dine with him, and he with Me.

Revelation 3:20